on the Internet

2nd edition

Andrew Kinsman

PUBLISHING

www.dandbpublishing.com

First published in 2003 by D & B Publishing, PO Box 18, Hassocks, West Sussex BN6 9WR

Second edition 2005

British Library Cataloguing-in-Publication Data
A catalogue record for this book is available from the British Library.

ISBN 1-904468-20-9

All sales enquiries should be directed to:
D & B Publishing, PO Box 18, Hassocks, West Sussex BN6 9WR, UK
Tel: 01273 834680, Fax: 01273 831629,
e-mail: info@dandbpublishing.com,
Website: www.dandbpublishing.com

Cover design by Horatio Monteverde.
Production by Navigator Guides.
Printed and bound in the US by Versa Press.

Contents

Preface to the Second Edition

It is only seven short years the first real money online poker site was created. In that time the online poker industry has developed into one in which the leading companies have annual turnovers of hundreds of millions of dollars. Tens of thousands of people already enjoy playing regular online poker and more and more are joining them every day.

The purpose of this book is to provide a thorough overview of online poker, which will benefit both newcomers and experienced players alike. It will address such frequently asked questions as: How do I choose an online poker room at which to play? How does online card-room play differ from 'live' cardroom play? Is there a risk of being cheated or colluded against? How can I use the Internet to improve my play? What newsgroups and other useful poker resources are available? ... and much more.

Although the book is designed to be useful to all poker players, most of the specific examples I have used relate to Texas hold'em, rather than to Omaha, seven-card stud or other games, since this form of the game is overwhelmingly the most popular online. In general, however, you will find that these examples apply equally as well to other games as they do to hold'em.

The very nature of the Internet is such that it is constantly changing and evolving. In view of this, this second edition has been fully revised to incorporate all of the recent major developments. When the first edition went to print in early 2003, the World Poker Tour TV series had not yet been broadcast, and Chris Moneymaker had yet to change the face of poker by winning the World Series of Poker. So much has happened in poker in the past two and a half years!

I am most grateful to Max Shapiro for kindly agreeing to allow the use of one of his *Card Player* articles in the book. In addition, I would like to thank Byron Jacobs, Cassandra Kinsman and Chris Rowsome for their helpful comments and corrections. Naturally, they are not responsible for any errors which remain.

I hope that you enjoy reading this book as much as I have enjoyed researching and writing it. Your feedback is welcomed at the e-mail address below.

Andrew Kinsman, July 2005
E-mail: andrew@pokerupdate.com
Website: **http://www.pokerupdate.com/**

Playing Poker Online –
What's the worst that could happen?

The following piece first appeared in Card Player *magazine (Volume 16, No. 5, 28 February 2003). It is reproduced here by kind permission of the author, Max Shapiro.*

'Let's go,' my sweetie said to me one evening as she cashed out. 'How did you do in your Omaha game?'

'Oh, not too bad,' I replied evasively.

'How much did you lose?' she demanded.

'Not much. A little over a hundred.'

'How much?'

'Well, maybe closer to two hundred. But that's not too bad.'

'In a $1-$2 game? You're impossible. With all my instruction, how come you always lose?'

'I don't know,' I said. 'It just seems like when the players see me coming, they rub their hands and run all over me.'

'Well, no wonder, with your reputation. Everyone knows you play like a wuss. I wish there were some way you could hide your identity.'

'How about I get plastic surgery?' I said sarcastically. 'Or maybe use a mask?'

'Those might work,' she said thoughtfully. 'But I've got a better idea. Why don't you try playing poker online?'

I looked around the casino. 'Play poker on line? I don't see any line.'

'Quit clowning. I meant on the Internet, where nobody knows who you are.'

'Everybody knows who I am,' I said indignantly. 'I'm America's foremost gaming humorist.'

'Oh, you're a riot, all right. Look, Maxwell, there are lots of good reasons to play online. You don't have to sit next to people who need baths, or watch people chewing food with their mouths open making disgusting noises.'

'Hey, that's right,' I said, beginning to warm to the idea. 'And I don't have to tip dealers, either.'

'Oh, sure,' she laughed. 'Think of all the quarters you'll save.'

'Hey, it all adds up.'

'The number of times you win a pot, I don't think you have to worry much about tipping,' she zinged me, getting in the last line, as usual. 'But the main thing is hiding your identity, because when you play online, you can use a fictitious name, like "Bust-Out", or "Worm", or something like that.'

'Yeah, how about "Max the Ax", or "Poker Ace"?'

'I think "Dead Money" or "Fishy-Fishy" might be more appropriate,' she responded. We finally compromised when I came up with a name that nobody could ever associate with me, and one that Barbara warned me never, ever, to reveal to anyone. It's "Mop-Top". Clever, aren't I?

I asked Barbara what I had to do next to play online. 'Buy a computer,' she said.

'I have a computer,' I protested.

'You call that relic a computer?' she laughed. 'Its memory is measured in kilobytes, it has the speed of a turtle on crutches, and it runs on Windows 1956.'

'Hey, I paid a lot of money for that computer.'

'You found it in a dumpster, Maxwell. Don't be so cheap and buy one that works.'

Again we compromised. I took it in to an electronics store, had extra memory put in, and even replaced two missing letters on the keyboard. What a waste of money! How often do you use the letters 'q' or 'z' anyway?

Before I started playing, I thought I'd do some research. I asked my friend John Bonetti, the famous but uncouth poker player, if he played online.

'Soitenly not!' he replied indignantly in his inimitable New York/Italian accent. 'What's the point of playin' poker when you can't coise the dealers? Fuhgetabout it, I got my standards.'

How could I be so thoughtless? Next, I ran into Big Denny, operator of the notorious Barstow Card Casino, and asked if he ever played on the Internet.

'Yeah, once,' he said. 'I seen dis ad what said dat if ya wanted, ya could play poker on da computer widout wearin' no clothes. So I tried it, an' ya know what — dey arrested me!'

'Wait a minute,' I said, thoroughly puzzled. 'You were undressed, playing poker in your own home on your computer, and they arrested you?'

Big Denny scratched his head. 'Dey didn't say nuttin' about playin' at home. I ain't got a computer, so I wuz playin' in one of dem Internet cafes.'

'Anyways,' he added, 'I wuzn't havin' no fun on account of ya can't t'row cards or peek at someone else's hand or do nuttin' like that.'

Well, so much for my research. I told Barbara I was ready to give it a go. We investigated various poker sites, and I chose one that offered games with 25- and 50-cent limits. It was called 'Piker Poker'. Following her instructions, I managed to log in and sign up for an Omaha game.

Checking out the table, I was intrigued by some of the names that players used, such as 'Pokerhontas', 'Stinkerbell', 'EmptySeat', 'ChipsyWoman', and 'AmarilloNotSoSlim'. I was studying them when a beeping sound went off.

'Is that the microwave oven?' I asked.

'No, you fool. That's a warning signal that your time is running out. It's on you.'

'What's on me?' I asked, brushing off my shirt.

'You've used that gag before,' my sweetie said in disgust. 'You have to act.'

'I'm supposed to act?' I stood up and started acting: 'To be or not to be.' 'Frankly, my dear, I don't give a damn.' 'Stella!'

As an alarm went off and I was timed out, Barbara threw up her hands. 'I give up. You're on your own, ace.'

'Well, fine! I can handle this myself just dandy without your meddling, thank you very much,' I said, though not loud enough for her to hear.

Getting back to Piker Poker, I examined the photos next to each player's ID. An adorable little blonde named Cupcake caught my eye. I began flirting harmlessly with her on the chat box, and our exchange of notes eventually resulted in a face-to-face meeting. To my dismay, I discovered that the names and photos were not always true-to-life. 'Cupcake' turned out to be a 900-pound truck driver.

Oh, well, I wasn't exactly being completely honest by calling myself Mop-Top and using a photo of a young Paul McCartney. But at least nobody could ever guess who I was.

I started playing, using my usual scientific Omaha strategy. Out of the first 45 hands, I folded 42 times before the flop, twice on the flop, and once I went all the way to fourth street. I was starting to get a little upset because I had played less than two hours and was already out $1.65. Even worse, the other players began posting insulting notes on the chat box.

'That rock plays just like Max Shapiro.'

'Nah, nobody plays that bad.'

'Hey, maybe it is Max Shapiro. Hey, Max, did your mommy give you some money to play poker?'

'I'll show them,' I vowed to myself. Sure enough, a hand later, I was dealt A-A-2-3 double-suited. I raised, which threw the table into shock, but five players called, and there were two more raises. The flop was a perfect A-5-4, which gave me a wheel and a set of bullets! There must have been some flush draws and other good hands out there, because the pot was capped and everybody called. A 4 on the turn gave me aces full along with my wheel. Another capped pot! On the river, incredibly, the pot was three-bet. I was about to make the final raise, which would have created an astounding, record-breaking $24 pot, when a horrendous message suddenly flashed on my screen: 'Your cheap computer has caused a fatal exception error. AOL will now shut down for upgrade and maintenance. You may be able to sign on again in a week. Thank you for using AOL.'

Frantically, I began trying to reach the Internet again. The start-up was infernally slow, and after finally getting online, I had to go through the process of signing in and finding my table at Piker Poker. When I finally got there, the hand was long over. I was left with 40 cents and a bunch of sniggering remarks in the chat box.

'Keep the 40 cents for a tip!' I wrote in a rage, and signed off.

Later, my sweetie asked me how I liked playing on the Internet.

'Easy pickings,' I replied. 'I had some bad beats, but I'll do better next time.'

Max Shapiro writes a humour column for Card Player, *the world's leading poker magazine, in which he irreverently explores the wackier side of poker using a motley mix of real and invented characters such as Big Denny, Dirty Wally, and Ralph the Rattler. He has also published a collection of these columns in a book entitled* Read 'em and Laugh. *A former journalist, Shapiro is semi-retired and lives in Hollywood, California.*

Chapter One

Introduction

'The first time I saw someone playing poker online, I couldn't believe it. I'm watching Mary, my normally quiet and reserved friend, jumping up and down in front of her computer, screaming. "I just beat someone from Hong Kong!" Right then, I realised the Internet would revolutionise poker.' Mike Caro – the 'Mad Genius of Poker'

What is Internet Poker?

In the past dozen or so years the Internet has transformed many aspects of our lives. E-mail, Instant Messenger and the World Wide Web have all had a major effect on how people communicate with one another and exchange information. The Internet has changed the way we shop, carry out research and entertain ourselves, so it is hardly surprising that it has an impact on poker as well. It has created a new frontier for the game, not only enabling players to exchange knowledge with one another, but also introducing a new medium for game play which has brought in thousands of new poker players and provided existing ones with much greater playing opportunities.

Although even players who have no wish to actually play online will find much of benefit on the Internet, it is the ability for players to compete against each other online that is by far the most significant development. Nowadays you can sign up at an online site, deposit funds into your account and, in a matter of minutes, be playing in real-time for real money against other people from all over the globe. The software handles everything: dealing, indicating whose turn it is to act, making sure that the correct amount is bet, determining the winner of the pot and assessing each player's wins and losses for that hand. The player merely has to focus on how best to play his hand!

The phenomenon of playing real-time poker online with other players began in earnest with Inter Relay Chat (IRC) poker back in the early 1990s. On IRC an automatic program handled the dealing and controlled the action, and various graphical interfaces were available to make the game more user-friendly. Naturally this was not 'real money' poker, but players still had a bankroll of 'etherbucks', which they carried forward from one session to the next. As was the case in many early Internet projects, the IRC pioneers enjoyed great camaraderie in breaking new ground and laying the foundations for online poker as we know it today. Although IRC poker enjoyed some popularity in the mid-1990s, the launch of real money cardrooms in the late nineties rapidly eroded its player base, and by the end of 2001 it was no longer operating.

In place of IRC, there are now over 250 online cardrooms of varying sizes, all vying with one another for a place in what is a multi-million dollar industry. The very nature of offshore gambling is such that any attempts to quantify its scale can only be approximates. However, it has been estimated by Dennis Boyko of pokerpulse.com that 1.82 million people played online poker in March 2005 (which represents a year on year increase of nearly 250%). According to European investment bank Dresdner Kleinwort Wasserstein, online poker revenues will reach around $2.9 billion in 2005, and will double in size by 2008.

Many of these people had never previously played poker in a casino or home game before they joined an Internet cardroom. However, having realised how much fun poker can be, a number of them have taken their new-found skills into brick and mortar cardrooms and become part of the next generation of live-action players. In this way Internet poker, while attracting a huge number of players in its own right, may also act as a kind of 'farm system' for live-action games. And of course many experienced live-action players have been attracted to the online game as well; some of them have even set themselves up as online professionals!

The primary goal of any cardroom is to generate rake income (typically in the form of a percentage taken out of each pot or a registration fee added to a tournament buy-in). The day-to-day challenge faced by each cardroom is building (and sustaining) a critical mass of players – the more full tables there are, the more the cardroom can expect to earn. Cardrooms may seek to bring in players through advertising, fast and reliable software, attractive promotions and efficient customer service. In many cases this is a virtuous circle – the more players there are who play at a site, the more players will want to play, drawn in by the fact that they can always find a game at their favourite limit or variation of poker. However, this circle can turn the other way as well, and poorly attended sites sometimes find themselves on a downward spiral. A loss of players can be self-perpetuating, since once a player has visited a few times without being able to find a game, he may well take his business to a site where he is guaranteed to be able to play.

The challenge for any poker site is to incorporate the key traditional poker elements that players are familiar and comfortable with, while at the same time taking advantage of the additional possibilities that the new medium provides. An effective online poker platform must have the ability to handle thousands of users at once, playing, chatting, joining and leaving tables, visiting the lobby, transferring funds to and from their accounts etc. However, just as important as volume is speed – people expect immediacy in their online experiences and quickly become disillusioned if they encounter persistent delays.

Most sites invest a substantial proportion of their rake income on advertising and marketing aimed at attracting new players and retaining existing ones, and some even employ 'prop' players to start up new games and hold up existing ones (see the section on 'Online Props' later in this book). Naturally, the major online cardrooms advertise in poker magazines such as *Card Player* and *Poker Europa*, and much of their budget is spent on banner advertisements at both general and poker-specific websites. Sometimes the banner host (or 'affiliate') is paid a monthly fee, but often remuneration is directly related to how many new clients are generated by the ad, with the host either receiving a flat fee for each new client or an ongoing share of that player's contribution to the rake. Indeed, it has been suggested that in general each new client that a site recruits initially costs them over $100.

Starting up a new online poker site is a far from straightforward operation. Apart from the expenditures involved in creating, maintaining and enhancing a poker software client, there are also major costs involved in hosting the game servers, marketing the site, employing a customer support team and other backroom staff, paying transaction charges, etc. Fast, reliable software, good customer support and extensive advertising are essential to the success of any new online poker site, but it also helps to have a 'killer' feature, which may be either a marketing device (such as the PartyPoker.com Million) or a software innovation (such as the powerful multi-table tournament software at PokerStars). However, the rewards of a successful launch are obvious – a share of an expanding billion dollar industry that is attracting more and more players every day.

A Brief Chronology of Online Poker

January 1994
First IRC hold'em program is released

August 1995
Internet Casinos Inc. launches the world's first online casino

August 1997
Planet Poker opens for play money games

January 1998
Planet Poker becomes the world's first real money Internet poker cardroom

September 1999
Paradise Poker opens for real money games

November 1999
Planet Poker deals its 2nd millionth hand

February 2001
Paradise Poker deals its 50th millionth hand

July 2001
Pokerspot ceases running online games

August 2001
PartyPoker opens for real money games
Paradise Poker deals its 100th millionth hand

December 2001
PokerStars opens for real money games

March 2002
Final of the first PartyPoker.com Million

May 2002
Highlands Club ceases running online games

June 2002
Paradise Poker deals its 200th millionth hand

July 2002
PokerStars runs first World Championship of Online Poker

November 2002
PokerStars organises world's first 1500-player online tournament

March 2003
World Poker Tour premieres on the Travel Channel. Debut series includes PartyPoker.com Million and UltimateBet Aruba Classic

May 2003
PokerStars satellite qualifier Chris Moneymaker wins World Series of Poker

June 2003
PartyPoker overtakes Paradise Poker to become the biggest online cardroom

October 2003
PokerStars announces that it is joining the World Poker Tour with its PokerStars Caribbean Adventure

January 2004
UltimateBet organises the first-ever million guaranteed online tournament

February 2004
PokerStars organises its one millionth tournament

May 2004
PokerStars satellite qualifier Greg Raymer defeats huge 2500+ field to win World Series of Poker

October 2004
Paradise Poker acquired by Sportingbet plc for around $300 million
PokerStars sponsors first-ever European Poker Tour

June 2005

PartyGaming launches on London Stock Exchange with market value of over $8 billion

July 2005

World Series of Poker attracts over 5,500 players, 1,116 of whom qualified online at PokerStars alone. Joseph Hachem wins $7.5 million first prize.

Paradise Poker announces first-ever million dollar freeroll tournament

Gambling on the Internet

One of the biggest challenges faced by the online cardroom industry is the fact that in many places Internet gambling is either already considered, or may one day be made, illegal. Indeed, many supporters of online poker are concerned that the already problematic legal situation in the US could become even worse over time. As poker and sports betting journalist Nolan Dalla stated in a December 2002 Internet radio interview on voiceofpoker.com: 'Most people who are involved in online gambling have to be very concerned about the climate in Washington now, because we are talking potentially about prohibition, about certainly making it very difficult to fund online accounts (which is already happening), maybe even criminalising online gambling activities.' Dalla firmly believes that governments should allow individuals to spend their discretionary income as they see fit, and that if they wish to participate in gambling then they should be free to do so. In fact, Internet gambling has already been legalised in more than 50 countries and jurisdictions around the world.

Although for most players, online poker is an enjoyable (and perhaps profitable) pastime, for some others it can have a damaging effect on their lives, perhaps leading to compulsive gambling and debt problems, and it is on these issues that many opponents of online gambling focus. What may be an enjoyable hobby for one person, could well be the ruin of another. The anonymity of online gambling may also enable children to become involved, perhaps using their parents' credit cards, whereas they would never be able to gain access to a brick and mortar cardroom. It has also been well documented that, leaving aside issues of gambling, the Internet can actually be addictive in itself. A recent study by Web-

Websense Inc. suggested that as many as 25% of employees feel that they are addicted to the Internet. The fact that online gambling sites are so easily accessible means that they are particularly dangerous for anyone with a gambling or Internet addiction.

Is it Legal to play Online Poker (in the US)?

The short answer to this question is: 'no-one really knows for sure'. Certainly those factions who are opposed to Internet gambling would like to see it outlawed completely, but whether or not the law as it stands is in their favour is a matter for conjecture. Furthermore, many people also believe that since poker is not a game of chance, but of skill, it should in any case be excluded from any legislation banning gambling on the Internet. As for the likelihood of being prosecuted just for playing online poker, Professor I. Nelson Rose, who is regarded as one of the world's leading authorities on gambling law, has stated that: 'No ethical lawyer would ever tell you to break the law. But I have not found one reported case, in the history of the United States and Canada, of a player being arrested for making a bet on the Internet.' ('Busted for Betting Online', 2001, available at his website gamblingandthelaw.com.)

The key piece of US federal legislation relating to Internet gambling is the Federal Interstate Wire Act, which was introduced in 1961 to prohibit the wire transmission of sports bets by organised crime. In March 2000 Jay Cohen, owner of the Antiguan-based World Sports Exchange (WSEX) online sportsbook, earned the unfortunate legal distinction of becoming the first American to be sent to jail for violating this Act with regard to Internet gambling. Cohen voluntarily returned to the US in order to stand trial, intending to prove that the Wire Act did not apply to the Internet. However, he was sentenced to 21 months in prison for taking sports bets by phone and over the Internet, which he began serving in October 2002. Meanwhile, his two partners remained in Antigua, where they continue to run their licensed and regulated business outside the reach of American justice.

Although the Cohen test case suggests that the Wire Act does apply to those involved in the business of Internet sports betting, this does not in itself necessarily mean that the practice of individuals playing poker online for money is illegal. In an edition of *Online Poker News* (published at cardplayer.com), practising criminal defence attorney Allyn Jaffrey makes a strong case for the argument that online poker is *excluded* from the Wire Act's reach, since the Act specifically prohibits *sports betting* and nothing else in its wording (a rationale that is backed up by Case Law and the fact that proposed amendments to the Act demonstrate that the legislators do not believe that it currently prohibits online gambling as a whole).

In addition, the only directly relevant Case on Point found specifically that the Wire Act does not apply to online gambling. In February 2001 a consolidated suit was brought against MasterCard by 33 gamblers who were trying to evade payment of their debts. Their claim was that credit card companies were violating the Wire Act by allowing them to use their cards to finance their online poker accounts, and that their debts were therefore illegal. However, the suit was thrown out by the judge on the basis that the Wire Act only applies to sporting events, and his decision was subsequently confirmed at the US Court of Appeal. In her article, Jaffrey also cites other examples which appear to demonstrate that in any case the Wire Act does not apply to individual bettors, only to people actually *involved in the business* of betting, in other words, the bookmakers and their associates.

Although Jaffrey's analysis suggests that the Wire Act itself does not to apply to online poker, it is also important to consider whether online poker violates any other federal or state laws. In fact, over the past few years the Nevada Gaming Commission has carefully scrutinised all the available evidence to determine whether or not it would be legal for them to license online gaming. However, the situation is so complex and unclear that, even with the help of some of the best legal minds in the state, the Commission has not yet been able to come to a definitive decision. The fact that there have been so few online gaming prosecutions reinforces the sense that (in most US states) online poker players may not be violating any laws. In another *Online Poker News* column Jaffrey observes that: 'Both the Clinton Administration and the Bush Administration have taken the position that gambling online violates federal law. Their opinions are not binding on any court and, in practical terms, the government has not been successful in its efforts to prosecute those involved in online gaming.'

In yet another of her excellent *Online Poker News* articles, Allyn Jaff-

Jaffrey makes the interesting point that one reason why play money games are available at every site, is so that the site can claim in good faith that it is inviting players who reside in places where online gambling is banned to participate only in its *play money* games. If those players then choose to participate in real money games, then that is a matter for the player and not the site, since when a player signs up they have to agree not to play for real money if they reside somewhere where it is illegal to do so. With the onus of responsibility on the player rather than the site, the latter is removed from the likelihood of prosecution. And of course, as we have seen, the chances of any individual actually being prosecuted merely for playing online poker are highly remote. Indeed, the US Attorney General's office has stated that it 'strongly oppose[s] any legislation that would seek to make the activity of mere bettors – those not involved in the business of betting and wagering – a violation of federal law.'

However, as Dalla warned in his radio interview, the climate in Washington is generally moving strongly against online gaming, and to some extent private enterprise is already conforming to this. In the past couple of years most major credit card companies (and PayPal) have taken the unilateral decision to block online gambling transactions. Partly this is out of fear of being held accountable for having abetted illegal gambling operations, and partly of potentially being left without redress against cardholders refusing to pay their gambling debts in the event of a change in the law. And it is not just credit card companies who are distancing themselves from online gaming: Yahoo!, the popular Internet portal, no longer accepts advertisements from Internet gaming operations.

However, not everyone in Washington supports the outlawing of Internet gambling. US Representative John Conyers Jr. (a Detroit Democrat) introduced a bill in late 2002 (albeit after the Senate had already adjourned, so in reality primarily to set the wheels in motion for 2003) to set up a commission to consider making Internet gambling completely legal, with a view to then being able to regulate it, tax it, and put appropriate consumer protections in place. As Conyers said in his press release, 'Such an approach would be more effective at weeding out bad actors and creating protections and safeguards in cyberspace gaming that exist in brick and mortar casinos.'

Nowadays, the revenue streams involved are so huge that there is a real incentive for governments to legalise and regulate online cardrooms in order to capitalise on potential tax income. And such a move would of course be welcomed by the major cardrooms, since it would enable them to move into the mainstream. In early 2005 two bills were actually passed at the North Dakota House of Representatives to license and regulate online poker. However, the bill failed to pass in Senate after the US Department of Justice warned that the proposed bills could be in violation of federal law. At the time of writing, it was not clear whether these bills could be revived at some point in the future.

Ironically, the main beneficiaries of the US Government's stance on online gambling have been the cardrooms themselves. It is inconceivable to imagine that PartyGaming would now be worth over $8 billion, were it not for the fact that the giant US gambling companies (such as Harrah's and MGM Mirage) been barred from operating in the online poker market. After all, over 85% of PartyPoker's players are from the US. And with hundreds of thousands of Americans playing poker online, how could a ban ever be enforced in any case?

Interestingly, in 2004 the World Trade Organisation ruled that the US was actually in breach of international trade agreements by attempting to prevent Antigua (home of UltimateBet etc.) from establishing itself as an Internet gambling centre for Americans.

Although the situation in the US is unclear, there are of course many countries in which online poker is not subject to any such ambiguities. In the UK, for example, individuals are free to engage in all kinds of online gambling activities if they so wish.

Account Funding

In the past couple of years it has already become something of a challenge for many online players to finance their accounts. Most major US credit card companies block online gaming transactions, and even if you are fortunate enough to still be able to deposit funds in your account via credit card, few companies will nowadays permit transactions in the opposite direction.

For a time, PayPal, the secure online payment service, was an almost ideal workaround for many players, enabling them to circumvent credit card restrictions by making credit card deposits at PayPal, and from there simply transferring the money to their online gambling accounts. According to Brian McWilliams in an article at wired.com, by June 2002 PayPal was associated with over 1,000 online gambling merchants who, paying higher than standard fees, accounted for as much as 8% of PayPal's total income.

However, events move quickly in the online world, and by July eBay had announced that once its planned $1.4 billion acquisition of PayPal had gone through, it would no longer allow Internet gambling trans-actions due to an 'uncertain regulatory environment surrounding online gaming.' Then in August, following an investigation by the New York State Attorney General into Paypal's service to online gambling merchants, PayPal agreed to pay a $200,000 penalty to the State of New York, and at the same time cease processing such payments from its New York members almost immediately. Although this action was taken in voluntary cooperation with the Attorney General, with no admission of having violated the law, it was by now inevitable that PayPal would soon cease allowing online gambling-related transac-tions altogether, which they did in November 2002.

With the demise of PayPal as a means of funding their accounts, many players have now switched to the Canadian-based NETeller as an al-ternative payment processor. Like PayPal, NETeller does not charge its customers for transfers to and from cardrooms (although it does charge for credit card deposits). Transfers from your NETeller account to a cardroom are instant, but it can take 48 hours or more to move money in the opposite direction, and transfers from your bank or credit card to NETeller can also take several days. In general, NETeller is an ideal place to store some of your bankroll, to either use as a top-up if your funds run low at a particular site, or to use for reload bonuses when they become available.

Although most online poker sites do now offer the facility to fund an account via NETeller, the overall range of merchants who accept NET-eller is still quite limited compared to PayPal, so it is less convenient as a payment method for non-gambling-related transactions. Naturally, this relatively high reliance on gambling means that NETeller would be particularly vulnerable to any future regulatory intervention.

One possible solution to the problem of payment processing is the concept of a central online poker bank. Such a bank would allow players a completely portable bankroll, allowing them to immediately buy-in and cash-out whenever and wherever they wished to play. From the cardrooms' point of view, a central bank might also be an attractive option, since they would stand to make substantial savings on their transaction processing fees.

When Online Cardrooms go out of Business...

Since Planet Poker launched the first real money poker site in 1998, dozens of other companies have tried to follow in its footsteps. Some of these early starters, such as Paradise Poker, Poker.com (now The-PokerClub) and Planet Poker itself, are still around today, but many others have fallen by the wayside, in some cases leaving a trail of angry clients in their wake.

In June 2000 the Highlands Club, endorsed by none other than the legendary Doyle Brunson, was launched for real money play. However, the site was plagued by software problems and at one point some Russian hackers managed to break into the software and see all the hole cards for a brief time (apparently, more than $10,000 in compensation was paid out to those clients who had been cheated, which came straight from the hacker's account, since they were detected before they were able to cash out). Despite a series of attractive promotions, an attempt at running a prop programme, and even a drastic reduction in rakes to a maximum $1.50 per hand, the site was never able to achieve a critical mass of players and folded in the spring of 2002. Although he had in fact asked for his endorsement to be removed after the site had changed ownership the year before, Doyle Brunson generously agreed to ensure that all outstanding claims were met in full.

Clients of the now defunct Pokerspot were nothing like as fortunate, as it now seems highly improbable that they will ever get their deposits back. Pokerspot launched with its own proprietary software in June 2000, and within six months had established a client base of over a thousand real money players. However, the site ran into serious difficulties in early 2001 when the payment provider it was using, Net Pro, had its assets frozen by Barclays Bank, apparently due to financial irregularities. Pokerspot quickly ceased operations and has never managed to resolve its payment processor problems. According to the company's former President, Russ Boyd, approximately $400,000 belonging to Pokerspot's clients remains outstanding to this day.

Another example of a site that quickly ran into insurmountable difficulties was the Costa-Rican based PokerCosmo. Launched in late 2001, PokerCosmo never managed to attain a large enough player base and by April 2002 it was still only operating a few real money tables at any one time. In May it then vanished overnight, with no server, no website, no support, and no realistic chance of clients ever seeing their deposits again.

In a recent post on the rec.gambling.poker newsgroup, Pokerspot's Russ Boyd offered the following advice to online players, based on his own experiences: 'Players should not treat these sites as banks. I would suggest that online players not leave their bankroll in them. Keep your bankroll in a bank and make a new deposit every time you buy into a table. Then cash out everything you have in your account regularly ...as often as the casino will let you ...We weren't the first and we won't be the last [to have gone down].'

Chapter Two

Live vs. Online Play

'It's not enough to have a girlfriend with a job and a credit card, I need to dump her and find one with a job, a credit card and a Pentium IV.'
Gary Carson, author of *Hold'em Poker*

Introduction

When you sit down at an online poker table, it is important to remember that it is just that, an *online* poker table – the card skills you may have learnt playing in live-action games will remain the bedrock of your game, but they need to be fine-tuned. Online poker is very much still poker, but it is poker in a very distinct form. The online poker room is a completely different environment to a home or brick and mortar cardroom game, and your success or failure at the tables will be determined as much by how well you adapt to this environment, as by whether you have the skills to beat a live-action game. Poker forums and newsgroups are littered with stories of live-action players who have come unstuck online, having failed to adjust to the peculiarities of this form of the game and left their hard-earned bankrolls in the hands of the online specialists. Fundamentally, success in online poker is more dependent on the cards you hold, your ability to make fast, accurate decisions and your own self-discipline, whereas in live-action poker, people-reading skills are relatively much more important.

Taking the First Steps

Once you have taken the decision to play online, the first key choice you must make is to select a site at which to play. All sites are not equal and it is well worth spending an hour or two visiting different sites and comparing what they have to offer (see also Chapter Four – 'Selecting an Online Cardroom'). Most major sites require you to download their software before you are able to play, but there also some sites that work through Java applets and therefore do not require a download. In general, most players prefer the download approach, since the time taken to download the software and install it on a hard drive is usually more than offset by the better graphics and performance of the download version. However, Java-based programs are particularly well suited to players who do not have access to the Windows environment, or are not permitted to install software on the computer at which they wish to play.

Once you have made your choice of site, it is a fairly straightforward matter to download the software (or applet). This software will contain a poker client which runs on your computer and talks to the online cardroom's poker server. All you need to do then is select a screen name (or 'handle') and sign up (don't forget to take a note of your username and password for next time!). At this point, you will usually be prompted to deposit some funds to your account. However, if you don't feel ready to start playing for real money straightaway, but first wish to familiarise yourself with the peculiar mechanics of the online game, you can skip this and go straight to the play money tables. It may seem a little strange at first, but once you have played three or four times you should become more comfortable with it. If your chosen site offers freeroll tournaments, then you may also wish to take advantage of these before deciding whether or not to deposit any cash funds to your account.

When you are logged-in at an online poker site, it is relatively straightforward to take up a seat at a table. You simply select a table by double-clicking on it in the lobby (if the table is full you will be given the option of placing yourself on the waiting list) and then when the table appears you simply double-click on an empty seat. At this point you are usually asked to select how many chips you wish to buy-in for (see the 'Managing an Online Bankroll' section of this book for a more detailed discussion of buy-ins) and then you are all set to go. After the current hand has been completed you will be prompted to either post a blind straightaway or postpone this until you arrive in the big blind position. In ten-player ring games some players actually prefer to post their first blind after the button has passed (from the position to the right of the button, often known as 'the cut-off') rather than in the big blind position, since they will then receive a number of 'free' plays before they arrive at the big blind.

Once you are dealt in, the software will prompt you when it is your turn to act and indicate how much you can bet, although you may elect to use the 'advance-action' (or 'in-turn') boxes if you have already decided what to do before your turn comes around. When you are settled into the game, you may elect to click on the 'auto-post blinds' option, so that your blinds are posted without causing any delay to the game. If you decide to sit out for a while (note that most sites only allow you to sit out for a maximum three rounds before removing you from the table) and then return to the game, you will have to pay any missed blinds, just as you would in a live-action game.

At some point you may decide to take the plunge and play for real money. Be sure to visit the relevant section of the poker room's website for instructions on this procedure. Essentially the process of depositing funds is not dissimilar to that of any other online purchase, but depending on your nationality and the gambling policy of your credit card company, you may need to make a credit card transfer to a third party handler such as NETeller, and then move the funds from there to your online poker account. If you do not possess a credit card then most sites allow you to deposit funds through some other means.

Many sites offer a deposit bonus for first-time customers, which can be as much as 25% of your initial deposit, transferable to your account once you have participated in a certain number of raked hands. It is well worth taking advantage of as many of these offers as you can, while you try out different cardrooms. These promotions are not available at every site, and can also change from time to time, so you will need to check their websites to see what deals are currently available. It is important to read the terms of the bonus offer carefully, since often you will be required to play a certain number of hands by a certain date, otherwise the bonus is deemed null and void.

Online cardrooms do place restrictions on the sums that may be deposited in a 24-hour period. Partly this is for the protection of their clients, to prevent players from overexposing themselves by making substantial deposits that could lead to financial ruin, but fundamentally it is to ensure that they themselves are protected from credit card fraud or contested charges.

Live vs. Online Play – The Differences

In this section we shall discuss the pros and cons of online play compared to live play. Broadly these can be broken down into: personal features, social features, financial features, game selection features and game play features.

Advantages of Online Play: Personal Features

1. You can play online in the comfort, safety and security of your own home.

Many people enjoy listening to music, watching sports in the background, or surfing the Internet while they are playing. Furthermore, there is no need to carry large sums of cash around, or for possibly long and tiring commutes to and from a casino.

2. Online play preserves your anonymity.

Some players would prefer that their friends, family and business associates are not aware that they play poker.

3. Online poker is less intimidating than a live-action game.

The Internet is not only a relatively safe and secure place to learn poker, but also a much less intimidating environment for most people than a live-action cardroom. In particular, many women seem to prefer to learn the game online, where they can avoid the possibility of being subject to the scrutiny of unsympathetic male players, and can focus on the game rather than on having to fend off unwanted male advances. Indeed Ladbrokes has reported that female players now represent 20% of the online poker population.

4. There is no dress code.

You can play in your pyjamas or shorts. Unlike at UK casinos, for example, 'smart casual dress' is not a requirement of entry to an online game.

5. You can play with a coach/friend alongside you.

Although poker is generally required to be 'one player to a hand', this is impossible to enforce online. Many people receive their first introduction to poker while they are sitting alongside an online player, receiving instructions and a practical demonstration of how to play.

Advantages of Online Play: Social Features

6. Sitting in a smoking/no-smoking environment is a personal decision.

Many non-smokers dislike playing in cardrooms due to the smoke; and many smokers have no choice but to play in no-smoking cardrooms. The Internet allows both smokers and no-smokers to play in their preferred environment.

7. You can avoid unpleasant opponents.

The nature of online play is such that there are fewer arguments, and you don't have to put up with boorish (or smelly) opponents moaning about bad beats. In the relatively rare circumstances that another online player decides to pick on you or one of the other players, there is almost always another game that you can play instead, or you can simply mute or ignore the chat box.

8. There are no players acting out of turn or breaching other rules of poker etiquette.

The very structure of the online game forces those players who might otherwise conform only very loosely to the rules of the game, to behave in the appropriate manner, acting in turn and within a certain standard amount of time.

9. You can quit whenever you want.

There is no social pressure to stay in the game when it is no longer 'good' or you become too tired to play your best. In a live-action game the other regular players may make snide comments if you quit with a large win or when the game is in danger of breaking up, whereas online you are never under any such obligation to continue playing.

10. You can run bluffs online that you would perhaps be too embarrassed to show down in a live-action game.

Online no-one can give you a dirty look or verbally criticise your play when you show up on the river with garbage on a stone-cold steal!

Advantages of Online Play: Financial Features

11. Online games have a lower rake and no tipping (and usually no jackpot rakes either).

The standard maximum rake for a full 10-player ring game online is $3 'no flop, no drop', whereas in many brick and mortar cardrooms it is $4 (or more) with an additional $1 often being added for the jackpot and a $1 (minimum) tip almost automatically paid to the dealer. For low-limit players in particular, a significantly smaller sum of money comes off the table in every hand online than would be the case in a live-action game.

12. You can play for smaller stakes online than in brick and mortar cardrooms.

It is hardly economic for brick and mortar cardrooms to offer games as low as $1/$2 (let alone $0.50/$1.00 or below), but such limits are an attractive training ground for new players seeking to learn the game without having to spend a fortune on their education. For this very reason, the $1/$2 and below 'micro-limit' online games are popular at all online sites. Indeed, even experienced players sometimes opt to play at a lower limits when they wish to work on a particular area of their game. For example, a $5/$10 brick and mortar player might choose to play online at a $2/$4 limit five-handed table in order to hone his short-handed skills. Furthermore, all online sites also offer play money games, which do not require any cash investment at all.

13. You can't accidentally muck a winner or lose a pot due to a dealer error online.

Again this feature is particularly attractive for novice players who might accidentally misread their hand or allow a dealer to muck their cards when they are holding a winner.

14. There are no travel expenses incurred in playing online.

For regular players who do not live in immediate proximity to a brick and mortar cardroom, travel expenses can amount to a significant sum over the course of a year.

15. Many online cardrooms offer attractive sign-up and other deposit bonuses.

Although many US cardrooms do reward regular players with 'comps', this is by no means standard, whereas many online sites offer 15%-25% bonuses on initial deposits, and often these bonuses are even extended to include existing clients in the form of 'reload' bonuses.

16. Online cardroom restrictions on deposits prevent players from using their credit cards to deposit and lose thousands of dollars in a single day.

Whereas most casinos will allow players to purchase chips up to their pre-agreed credit limit, and individuals may also be able to obtain additional funds from ATM machines or fellow players, online cardrooms prevent players from making substantial credit card deposits in a single day. Indirectly, this thereby enforces a 'cooling-off' period before they can return to the game.

17. Some online cardrooms allow ratholing of profits.

Some pot-limit and no-limit players like to remove their profits from the table if they are on a small bankroll, buying straight back in for the minimum and 'ratholing' the rest to protect it. This practice of removing chips from the table is considered poor etiquette and is rarely allowed in brick and mortar games, but online cardrooms do permit it, although some do place a time limit of 30 minutes or more before allowing players to return to the game with anything less than the sum with which they departed. (Naturally, ratholing might be considered an unattractive feature if someone is removing your money from the table!)

Advantages of Online Play: Game Selection Features

18. There is always an online game available somewhere 24/7.

Whatever time of day it is, in whatever part of the world you are (and however far you are from a brick and mortar cardroom), you can always find an online game in which to play – all you need is a computer, a reliable Internet connection and an account with some funds in it! It is not necessary to wait for an hour or more online to obtain a seat, as is sometimes the case at peak times in some popular brick and mortar cardrooms. Furthermore, you can play online when you only have maybe 15 minutes or half an hour to spare, rather than having to devote a whole evening to playing poker.

19. There is a greater range of limits and tournaments (including many freeroll events) online.

Whereas most brick and mortar cardrooms offer a relatively small range of limits and perhaps one or two (if any) tournaments a day, there is a sufficiently wide range of games online that you can choose to specialise largely in tournaments, short-handed or heads-up play, pot-limit Omaha hi/lo or whatever else may take your fancy.

20. You have a wider choice of opponents online.

Depending on the time of day and the limit involved, there are often several games available at the same limit, so you can select the best one according to your preferred criteria. Furthermore, once you are playing, it is easy to change tables should you decide that there is a better opportunity elsewhere.

21. Online play offers a greater range of cardrooms to choose from.

Outside of California and Las Vegas, few brick and mortar players have the luxury to pick and choose between cardrooms, whereas online there are a countless number to select from. Many online players have accounts with several different sites, which enables them scout around for the best games at the click of a button.

22. Most online sites offer the facility to play simultaneously at two or more tables.

In a brick and mortar cardroom you are naturally restricted to one table, playing maybe 30 or so hands per hour. However, online you can be seated at several tables at once, conceivably playing 200 or more hands per hour if you so wish.

Advantages of Online Play: Game Play Features

23. Online, the software guides you through the game, telling you when to act, what the action is up to that point, and how much you can bet.

Whereas newcomers to a brick and mortar cardroom may find the structure of the game a little bewildering, perhaps being intimidated by the fear of acting out of turn or failing to bet the correct amount, the online game is a lot more straightforward for beginners. Online players are prompted automatically when it is their turn to act, and presented with a list of the betting options available.

24. Online you always have clear information on everyone's stack sizes, the pot size and the size of any side pots.

Whereas in live play it is easy to lose track of the exact size of the pot and perhaps not be able to see how many chips a player has left, this information is provided in clear fashion in the online game.

25. Online games are much faster than live-action ones.

A computer can collect, shuffle and deal cards far faster than a human can, and there are no delays caused by the need to wait to change decks or dealers (or take a table charge), while there is also no reliance on a human dealer to work out who has won a pot or manage the chip division in a split pot. In addition, players generally act much faster online, since no-one has to count out their chips to place into the pot, and players can use 'fold in turn' and other advance-action boxes to speed up the game. Since there are no visual tells available, the game is also not slowed down by players looking around the table for clues on other player's hands. Consequently, the faster sites are able to deal at least two to three times as many hands per hour as their brick and mortar counterparts, and even more for short-handed games.

26. You don't need to keep a 'poker face' online.

Unlike in a brick and mortar game, there is no necessity to conceal your emotions when you play online. You can jump up and down cheering when you hit a flop without giving away the strength of your hand, since the other players will be none the wiser. Conversely, you can shout and scream at your computer when someone draws out on you on the river, and no-one else will have any idea that you might be 'steaming'.

27. Online shuffling results in a more random card distribution than can typically be achieved by a dealer.

Properly programmed computer shuffling software enables a fair and random shuffle without the appearance of clumps of the same cards, as can occasionally arise in live games. Furthermore, there is no risk that the dealer might rig the shuffle, accidentally flash a card or mis-deal altogether, or of other players being able to mark the cards.

28. Most online cardrooms provide the facility to review hand histories, and also offer note-taking facilities and statistics.

Once a hand has been played and mucked in a brick and mortar card-room, there is rarely any accurate record of what occurred. However, online hand histories enable players are able to go back and review the hand, analysing both their own play and that of their opponents with a view to finding ways in which to improve their game. Many dedicated online players also choose to take advantage of the note-taking facilities and statistics functions that most online cardrooms provide.

29. An online cardroom can review the record of every hand for possible cheating.

The hand history facility also allows cardrooms to go back and look at hands after they have been played, either to check for any possible collusion or to resolve any other issues that may have arisen. Once a hand has been irretrievably mucked in a live-action game, on the other hand, it is often impossible to reconstruct what occurred with perfect accuracy.

Disadvantages of Online Play: Personal Features

1. There is a temptation to play online when you shouldn't.

Internet poker is so easily accessible that it is easy to find yourself playing when you would be better advised not to (during or after a drinking session, for example). While it is true that alcohol is permit-ted in most live-action games, you are less likely to run into someone who is playing poker completely drunk in live play than you are online. On occasion, some online players even take the time and trou-ble to inform others at the table of exactly how much they have drunk! (If you come across such a player, please feel free to e-mail me so that I can join the party.)

2. There are more distractions when playing online than in a brick and mortar cardroom.

The fact that most people play online in their homes, means that potentially they could be distracted by other matters and, in failing to pay full attention to the table, start to make mistakes. Whereas in a brick and mortar game, the physical presence of other players should be enough to keep your attention on the game, this safety net is absent from the online game. Most online players are, to a greater or lesser extent, guilty of answering e-mails, surfing the Internet or watching TV while they are playing. (It follows that you will have an instant edge over many of your less focused opponents if you simply give the game your full attention. Online poker is real – the players are real and the money is certainly real!)

3. Like all 'computer games', online poker may encourage obsessive and compulsive behaviour in some people.

The relatively easy accessibility of online poker might be potentially very damaging for 'problem gamblers', since the next opportunity to gamble is only a mouse-click away. Furthermore, it is easy to get sucked into playing 'just one more hand' or 'just one more round' and before you know it another hour has passed by.

4. Online poker is a very untactile form of the game.

Most players prefer the tactile qualities of physical cards and chips to making impersonal movements of a mouse around a screen. Indeed, some players like to hold a few chips in their hands while they are playing online, in order to make the game seem more 'real'.

5. Online poker could potentially have negative health effects.

For players who play for many hours each day (like anyone else who spends a great deal of time on a computer) there is the risk of RSI or other computer-related health problems such as eye strain and headaches. Furthermore, nowadays many people already spend their working hours at a keyboard, and it may be unhealthy or unsatisfying for them to spend their free time at a computer as well.

Disadvantages of Online Play: Social Features

6. There is little social interaction online.

For many players the general social interaction of a brick and mortar game is one of its most appealing qualities. If you attend a regular weekly game, for example, you have the opportunity to chat with old friends and share the odd joke while you are playing. Although all online cardrooms offer a chat facility, this is a poor substitute for proper conversation. Professional players who play exclusively online may therefore experience a sense of social isolation.

7. There is no face-to-face psychological warfare.

Many brick and mortar players enjoy the fact that they are engaged in combat with other players sitting nearby; human beings whom they can look straight in the eye, rather than pixelated representations on a computer screen.

8. There are no waitresses bringing food and drink online.

If you need beer or pizza you actually have to get up and fetch it yourself!

Disadvantages of Online Play: Financial Features

9. There is no internationally recognised regulation of online gaming operations.

Many players are understandably wary of depositing substantial funds with online cardrooms. Apart from fears over the legality of playing online poker for real money, there are two main reasons for their concerns. First, if the cardroom were to go out of business, they would most likely lose any funds that are being held on account. And second, if they became involved in a dispute with the cardroom, their account might be frozen without any means of legal redress.

10. It is more problematic to buy-in and cash-out online.

In a live-action game you can just show up with the cash and sit down to play, whereas online poker requires that players have some electronic means of funding their account. Likewise, you cannot simply walk away from an online game with a bundle of notes, but will experience a delay of at least a few days while any cash-out is processed. One side-effect of this is that there are fewer purely casual players online than in a casino – the hassle involved in buying in online is enough to deter anyone with only a passing interest in poker from playing solely on a whim.

11. Online games have a higher hourly variance than live play.

Online players generally experience higher hourly swings than their live-action counterparts. This extra volatility can be attributed primarily to the greater number of hands that are dealt per hour in an online game. However, experienced brick and mortar players may also encounter greater variance because they are deprived of the visual tells which usually enable them to save a few big bets or win an extra pot or two in each session.

12. There is potentially more chance of going on tilt online.

It is more important (and harder to maintain) your emotional control and general discipline when there is no-one else around. The very fact that they do not want to embarrass themselves in public, is enough to prevent many players from going on tilt in a live-action game. However, there are no such emotional checks in place when you play online, and the fact that you are playing with 'cyber' chips rather than real chips may accentuate the problem. Furthermore, the online game is so fast that you can find yourself on tilt before you know it.

13. Online games are generally regarded as tighter than live-action games.

On the whole, online players are more poker-obsessed and poker-literate and will therefore play in a tighter fashion than their brick and mortar counterparts (for some of whom poker is more a social event, possibly being combined with a visit to the blackjack table, some slots and a little roulette). Indeed, many good players choose to play at lower limits online than they would in a live-action cardroom; the speed of the online game and the fact that they can play multiple tables means that they can earn as much (or more) online than they would in their normal brick and mortar game.

Furthermore, most online opponents are competing at a level with which they are comfortable, and not being forced to play out of their depth just because it was the only seat available. In online play, casual or inexperienced players can choose to play at micro-limits, whereas in brick and mortar cardrooms they would very likely be forced to play at least at $3/$6 or $5/$10 limits. The micro-limits provide these new players with the opportunity to learn to play poker very cheaply before they venture into the online low-limit and middle-limit games. In addition, many of the looser players who provide the 'action' in full ring brick and mortar games, opt for short-handed rather than full games online. Finally, weak online players are usually prevented from going on serious tilt for thousands of dollars, due to online credit restrictions. Instead of losing whatever may be in their wallet, without ever having to add it up, these players are forced to establish a proper bankroll when they buy-in.

Disadvantages of Online Play: Game Selection Features

14. You cannot change seats online without leaving the table and therefore possibly losing your seat altogether.

Brick and mortar cardrooms always provide players with the option of moving seats when another player leaves, but in an online game you cannot change seats in this fashion. You must first leave the table and then buy back in, which would place you at the bottom of any waiting list.

Disadvantages of Online Play: Game Play Features

15. You may be disconnected from the site while you are playing.

Every online player occasionally experiences the frustration of disconnections from a site in the middle of a hand, either for Internet connectivity reasons or because of a local problem with their computer.

16. You need to be able to make good decisions more quickly online.

The online game is much faster and more frenetic. In fact, some experienced players deliberately act bewilderingly fast in order to confuse their opponents and perhaps cause them to rush their decisions.

17. It is more difficult to identify and use tells online.

Although (as we shall see later in the book) there are tells in the online game, these are far fewer and generally less reliable than tells in brick and mortar games.

18. It is more difficult to identify the really bad players quickly.

When a new player joins a table at a brick and mortar cardroom, it is often relatively easy to identify how experienced they are by the way they handle their chips, whether they act promptly in turn, the conversations they have with the dealer and other players, etc. (although it is true that some players do pretend to be inexperienced to deceive their opponents). However, online you have to rely solely on your interpretation of how they are playing their cards. Sometimes a new player to an online game might appear to be very loose, when in fact they have just received a glut of good starting hands. If you were instead able to see them in the flesh you would have immediately been able to peg them more accurately as a solid, experienced player.

19. In the online game there is a risk that players are either colluding by phone or Instant Messenger or perhaps cheating in other ways.

Although collusion does occasionally occur in brick and mortar games, it is much easier to collude online. Indeed it is even possible for one person to be playing two or more hands at the same table. This area is dealt with in detail in the section on 'Cheating' in Chapter Three.

Does Online Play help or hinder your Live Play?

For most of the new generation of poker players, their first experience of poker is increasingly likely to have come from playing online rather than in a live game. They may eventually switch to playing in live-action games (or combining live with online play), but their initiation to the game will probably have come online, where they don't have to worry about the etiquette of a live-action game or whether they are giving off tells to the other players. As and when these players do migrate to live play, it will inevitably take them a while to adapt to the different nature of this form of poker, and most of these players will initially struggle at the hands of regular live-action players. Many live-action players therefore see the online game as a potential source of future profits, not because they choose to play online themselves, but because it may bring a wave of relatively inexperienced players into their own games.

However, it is not just inexperienced players who often struggle to adapt from online to live play – many regular online players have complained that when they return to playing in a live cardroom their results are much worse. There are a number of reasons why this could be the case. For example, in a live game:

♠ They become distracted by the social aspect of the game, chatting to other players rather than focusing carefully on the game.

♠ They don't pay enough attention to the tells that are offered by their opponents.

♠ They don't pay enough attention to the tells that they themselves are offering their opponents.

♠ They don't recognise that their opponents are paying much more attention to the game than an online player generally would.

♠ They don't keep track of the pot accurately (whereas online this information is provided for you). Consequently some of their live plays are mistakes relative to the pot odds they are receiving.

♠ They become impatient due to the smaller number of hands that are dealt per hour in a live relative to an online game.

♠ They have become accustomed to playing more hands than they should when they are online, perhaps due to the generally loose nature of micro-limit play. If those same hand selections are retained when they switch to a live-action game, it is likely that their results will suffer.

♠ They don't vary their play sufficiently (since in online play it is comparatively less important to vary your play).

♠ They may play so rarely in a live game that their results are nothing more than a reflection of the inherent variance involved in playing poker.

If you plan to play in both live and online games it is important to do both regularly, since otherwise your skills in one or other area may decline due to lack of practice. As a general rule, micro-limit online players should be looking to play tighter in a live game than they would do online.

Online Poker for a Living

'How do you get a professional poker player off your porch? Pay him for the pizza!' – Poker adage

In the past few years a new generation of poker players has emerged: the online professionals. There is something very appealing for most people about the idea of playing poker professionally from the comfort of their own home, making their own hours and not having to answer to anyone else. And indeed, online pros do enjoy numerous advantages that their live counterparts do not. For example:

- ♠ They can find a game 24/7. Nor is it necessary for them to be in reach of a casino – all they require is a computer and an Internet connection.

- ♠ They are dealt many more hands per hour, with a cheaper rake and no need to tip the dealer (and no travel expenses as well).

- ♠ They can play multiple tables (possibly even at different sites) at once.

- ♠ They do not need quite such accurate people-reading skills. Online poker is much more a game of understanding cards and betting patterns than of deciphering tells. Online professionals also need not fear giving off tells themselves.

- ♠ They can spend time studying precise hand history records to determine their own strengths and weaknesses and those of their opponents.

- ♠ They can specialise in short-handed play (where the skill differential between strong and weak players is maximised) if they so wish.

Set against this, the downside of playing online professionally is that it is impossible to cash-out instantly from an online site, and online professionals may also experience a sense of social isolation from sitting in front of their screens playing poker day after day. Despite these disadvantages, online poker is an attractive means of earning money for many regular players. Indeed, there are hundreds of players who play online for such long periods every day that it must be their primary source of income, and thousands more who rely on online poker to earn a secondary income in their spare time.

The issue of how much online players might expect to earn is a very topical one on the various poker forums and newsgroups. In *Poker Essays*, Mason Malmuth discusses the issue of earnings expectations in some detail. He estimates that for $3/$6 hold'em an okay player *at that level* would probably be earning $4 per hour, a good player $8 and a great player $12. In full 10-player ring games online you can probably estimate that you are playing at least twice as many hands per hour as you would in a live-action game (on which Malmuth's figures are based). On that basis you could say that a great player at the $3/$6 might expect to earn $24, or four big bets per hour, playing a single table.

However, online players do not have the same opportunities to read their opponents (i.e. tells), so for online play a figure of two to three big bets per hour is probably about right for a great player at that particular limit, with good players earning anything between one and a half and two big bets per hour and decent ones between one and one and a half big bets per hour. At higher limits than $3/$6, there will be less overall discrepancy in the general level of play, so the hourly big bet earnings ratio will decrease as you move up in limits. For example, it is hard to imagine that there are too many $20/$40 players who are capable of sustaining a long-term hourly profit much in excess of $100 playing exclusively on a single 10-player table.

Chapter Three

The Fundamentals of Online Poker

'The advent of online players should certainly create a larger base of poker players throughout the world. Brick and mortar casinos will benefit from this growth, and that is good for the entire industry.' Mike Sexton, WSOP bracelet-winner, World Poker Tour commentator and PartyPoker host

Starting out in Online Poker

'In order to learn any game, you have to find the best players and play with them.' Johnny Moss, three-time WSOP Champion

All you really need to start playing poker online is a computer (ideally with at least 128Mb RAM) and an Internet connection (high-speed broadband is naturally preferable to a dial-up connection, but the latter should be fine, albeit a little slower). Every online poker site offers the facility for play money tables, at which players can practise their skills without having to risk real hard-earned cash. If you are a newcomer to online poker, you may like to try out one of these games to familiarise yourself with the mechanics of the game. Indeed, if you have never played poker before it is certainly advisable to experiment with these practice games before risking any hard-earned cash, in order both to get used to how the dealing and betting processes work, and to develop basic playing skills such as hand selection and the ability to read the board.

Although these free games are ideal for beginners, for most players their attraction quickly palls. Without the constraints created by having to invest real money, there is no incentive for players to fold, since anyone who busts out can simply request a new stack of play chips. Invariably there are one or two players who attempt to cap the betting on every round with little or no regard for hand selection, so that the game can often become a 'no fold-em hold'em' free-for-all, bearing little relation to real money poker.

There is unquestionably a skill element involved in being successful in play money games, but whether those skills are of any particular use in 'real' poker is a moot point. Whereas in real money games, one of the most important abilities that players need to develop is hand selection; practice games encourage players to do precisely the opposite! Likewise it is impossible to develop hand-reading or pot odds skills when most of your opponents are taking their hands to the river on marginal values. Furthermore, many of the strategic tools that are important in real money games (such as raising or check-raising to narrow the field) are almost irrelevant in play money games, where some players will call anyway, whether it costs them a single bet or three.

Both micro-limit ring games and $1 entry fee (and freeroll) tournaments, such as those at PokerStars, provide far more instructional value than play money tables. These games provide an ideal, inexpensive introduction to the game – everyone is playing for something real and consequently the quality of play in these events far outstrips that of a typical play money game. Furthermore, the fact that the online game is so much faster means that newcomers can develop their skills that much quicker, playing more hands in an hour of online play than they would in two hours at an ordinary cardroom. And of course, if you are prepared to watch and learn, every major site will allow you to sit out and observe their higher-stakes games, thereby potentially gaining a valuable free insight into the skills of the better players.

Online Game Selection

'I believe that the single most important decision in any form of poker is game selection; determining which cards to enter a hand with runs a close second.' Lou Krieger, author of *Hold'em Excellence* and *More Hold'em Excellence*

Whereas most live-action players (outside of California and Las Vegas) have a very restricted choice of possible games, the range of games on offer online is immense. Instead of driving to a cardroom, placing your name on the $5/$10 list and taking a seat when it becomes available, online you can choose between several limits, with many sites even offering several simultaneous games at the same limit. With so many different games to choose from, selecting the right opportunity becomes a much more important aspect of the game. Indeed, for players at $5/$10 and above, in particular, the consistent ability to identify good games in which to play have a significant effect on your bottom line at the end of the year – game selection becomes that much more important as you move up in limits.

Finding your Limit

The first and most fundamental aspect of game selection is identifying the correct limit at which to play: one that is commensurate with your abilities and bankroll; not so high that you feel intimidated, and not so low that you become bored and fail to play your best game.

In general, the standard of opposition will rise as you move up in limit, since you would hardly expect someone with the ability to beat a $10/$20 game to be playing in a $1/$2 game; it would simply not be worth their while. However, it is sometimes argued that some of the players in the $30/$60 game at PartyPoker are considerably weaker than those that frequent the $5/$10 game. One possible explanation for this is the fact that some $30/$60 players may be very wealthy and are naturally drawn towards the higher limits to make the stakes meaningful, regardless of whether they possess the requisite poker skills or not.

In contrast, the $5/$10 games at PartyPoker are neither big enough to provide excitement for these wealthy 'action' players, nor small enough to appeal to poker newcomers, most of whom will naturally choose to begin their apprenticeship at $3/$6 and below. Furthermore, some winning $30/$60 brick and mortar players may choose to play at lower limits online for reasons of trust, fearing the possibility of collusion.

Thus sometimes the $5/$10 PartyPoker games are filled with solid, experienced players who lack the bankroll or confidence to play at higher limits. Having said all that, the nature of poker is such that successful players do gravitate towards the higher limits, so the very best online players can nearly always be found playing at the highest limits available.

In a fairly recent (2001) *Card Player* article Nolan Dalla put forward the interesting theory that 'the highest-limit games do not necessarily equate to the greatest potential win amount.' He claims that over the years he has made far more money playing in the second-highest game in a brick and mortar cardroom than the highest, and in such circumstances he will often prefer a $10/$20 game to a $20/40 game. His theory rests on the following arguments:

♠ The highest-limit game will usually contain the best players at the cardroom.

♠ The highest-limit game may contain players who would usually play even higher if such a game were to be spread.

♠ The second-highest game will often contain a cross-section of players, including players who are not good enough for the higher game and those who are stepping up from low-limit games to 'take a shot' at a higher limit.

♠ The second-highest game will usually contain more 'loose-passive' players than the highest game, and this absence of aggression (with many players seeing the flop without a raise) is, he believes, exactly what you should be looking for in a game.

Dalla concludes that 'A winning player can make just as much playing one limit lower than his normal game – providing that the players are considerably weaker.' Instead, many players become tied to their ego, believing that it would be a step backwards to play in, to use his example, a $10/$20 game when they usually play higher. Don't fall into this trap – by all means strive to find the 'ideal' limit for your ability and bankroll, but at the same time you should be flexible enough to move up or down depending upon the specific game selection opportunities available at that particular time.

Choosing your Opponents

'If they're helpless and they can't defend themselves, you're in the right game.' Mike Caro

If game selection is the single most important decision in poker, then opponent selection is undoubtedly one of the most significant factors in making that decision. If you play regularly at the same limit at a single site, then you will often run into the same opponents whom you have faced before. At one of the smaller sites, you should be able to identify the good and bad regular players quite quickly, whereas at a larger site there will probably be a number of unfamiliar players in almost every game (set against this, the larger site will have the wider selection of games overall).

Whatever site you choose to play at, if you take the trouble to take notes while you play, you will quickly be able to identify whether there are any players whom you would particularly like to play against, choosing one table over another in order to target the weaker players and avoid the stronger ones. Sometimes it is even worth stepping up or dropping down in limit if you spot one or two of your favourite opponents playing in a higher or lower game than you would normally play. Often a game can be good even if it features just a single player who is almost guaranteed to lose all of his money.

But what if you don't know anything about any of the players, how do you then decide to play at one table rather than another? In that case you may choose to sit out and watch a few games to see which might be most suitable. If you are playing regularly at the higher limits of a particular site, games in which you don't recognise anyone can actually be potential goldmines, absent all the regular pros and perhaps instead filled with inexperienced players.

Many players, however, like to get stuck into the action as soon as possible. Instead of actually watching the games, they make their game selection according to the lobby information on the average number of players per flop (or fourth street for stud) and average pot size, if such information is provided by the site. Broadly speaking, games can be classified as follows:

High flop seen percentage and *high* average pot size: loose-aggressive

High flop seen percentage and *low* average pot size: loose-passive

Low flop seen percentage and *high* average pot size: tight-aggressive

Low flop seen percentage and *low* average pot size: tight-passive

Depending upon your style of play, one type of game may be more attractive than another. Some aggressive players often prefer tight-passive games, where they can use their forcefulness to steal more pots both before and after the flop, whereas many other players prefer loose games with normal-sized pots, where they do not have to pay too much to see the flop, but figure to be able to outplay their opponents from the flop onwards. Bear in mind, however, that it is very hard to beat a tight-aggressive game.

In general (using $3/$6 and $5/$10 online games as an example; micro-limit games will usually be somewhat looser), any game with more than 30% of players seeing the flop is certainly not prohibitively tight, and a figure of 40% or more indicates a very good game. An average pot size of around six big bets is fairly typical, and a pot of eight big bets or more is certainly on the large side.

However, you should exercise some caution with such selection methods, since with so many players coming and going online, the complexion of a game can change very rapidly with the arrival or departure of one or two loose players, either once you are involved in the game itself, or even just while you are sitting on the waiting list!

For example, it is not uncommon for tables with high flop seen percentages to attract long waiting lists as the vultures sense blood and start to circle, ready for the kill; by the time you reach the top of the waiting list they may have already devoured their prey and the game may no longer be good. Furthermore, it is possible that the current averages are not really a good reflection of the game as a whole – the inherent short-term fluctuations of a game of poker are such that the last 20 or so hands may not necessarily be a particularly reliable sample.

If you do decide to use the average players/flop or average pot statistics in game selection, it is important to check back to the lobby at periodic intervals to ensure that the game still meets your criteria.

Another factor that you may like to consider when making your table selection is the stack sizes of all the players. Whereas in a brick and mortar cardroom buy-ins can vary hugely from one player to the next, online they tend to be much more standardised. For example, if the maximum buy-in in a pot-limit game is $100 and there are three or more players with stacks of over $300 then you may be up against some quality players (or at least some players on a hot streak) who have been busting out their opponents, whereas if everyone has $50 or less then there is probably less to fear.

In a fairly recent (2002) article at casino.com, Andrew Glazer suggested that a similar concept may also apply to low-limit games. If there are several players with substantially larger stacks than the cardroom's 'recommended' buy-in for that limit, this may indicate that they are better than average players. Whilst this is obviously less reliable for limit than for pot-limit games (since in limit games some players like to buy-in for more than the recommended amount anyhow) it may still help to lead you away from the tougher games. However, Glazer's theory is probably more reliable when you are considering a table in which only one or two players are playing with even the recommended buy-in and the rest are short-stacked, either because they have already incurred losses (either through bad play or bad luck) to recently departed winners, or because they are inadequately bankrolled and were forced to opt for a short buy-in from the outset. In these circumstances, you can be fairly certain that at least the game is not full of sharks!

Finally, it is worth mentioning one final game selection 'shortcut' – you could just look for a player whom you know focuses carefully on game selection and join the game in which they are already playing!

The Rake Factor

One factor that many low-limit players overlook when considering which game to play is the rake. As a general rule, the rake becomes better value as the game becomes looser (or the stakes increase). Let's take the example of an online $5/$10 game in which the rake is extracted in typical fashion as follows: $1 for a $20 pot, another $1 for a $40 pot and a further $1 when the pot reaches $60. Let's say that a sequence of five pots in a row reach $60, hitting the $3 cap. If those pots were exactly $60 each time then the house would be extracting 5% of every pot, but in a looser game in which those same five hands each reached $90 the rake would only be 3.33% per hand.

This may not sound like much, but an increase of 1% or more in profit on every hand won over the course of a lifetime of playing poker would add up to many (and quite possibly tens of) thousands of dollars. In the long run, the percentage of each winning hand that an average low-limit player has to pay in rake could make the difference in determining whether or not they are an overall winner. Unless your style of play is innately better suited to tighter games, you should therefore tend to head towards the looser games, in which you will pay proportionately less rake over time, particularly since looser games with weaker players are generally easier to beat in the first place.

In the summer of 2002 the Swedish-owned 24hpoker.com launched its new poker site with an initial cap of $1.35 (plus $0.15 for the jackpot) on pots of $100 or less, in a direct challenge to the existing sites' standard of a $3 cap. However, this experiment failed to precipitate a 'rake war', and the more established sites did not see fit to respond by reducing their own rake caps. Partly, this is because at the low-limits that many online players participate, many games never reach the standard $40 threshold at which the second dollar of rake is actually taken.

Take your Seats

'If you can't spot the sucker in your first ten minutes at the table, then the sucker is you.' – Poker adage

Once you have selected a table at which to play, it is important to consider where you should sit. Often you will have no choice in the matter – there will only be one seat available and you will either have to take that place or go to the back of the waiting list. However, on other occasions you will be presented with a choice of two or more seats. Which criteria should you consider when selecting a seat?

If you know nothing about any of your opponents, there is little on which to base your decision. In those circumstances, many players recommend sitting to the left of where the majority of chips are located. In flop games, chips tend to move in a clockwise direction and, other things being equal, it is worth taking up a position that seeks to exploit this trend.

Your initial seating decision becomes more involved if you know the playing styles of some of your opponents. In those circumstances, the conventional wisdom is to sit to the left of the more aggressive players, with more passive players to your left. That way you can see the action of the aggressive players before you commit to the pot, and do not have to be too concerned about being raised every time you make a bet or call. You can thus take advantage of your position relative to the aggressive players, whilst the passive players can be counted on not to take full advantage of their position over you. In addition, if there is an opponent who calls nearly every hand pre-flop (in unraised pots), you would ideally like them on your right. That way whenever you have a premium hand you can almost guarantee that they will be investing two bets before the flop, one for their initial call, and another when they call your raise.

However, if there is a hyper-aggressive player who bets and raises at nearly every opportunity at the table, then the situation becomes a little more complex. It may be that you actually want them to your left – the fact that they are so predictable reduces the importance of holding position over them, since you can tailor your play so that whenever they are in the hand they can help bet your hand for you. The problem with having such a player on your right is that whenever they bet or raise you always have to act without knowing the actions of the players behind you – even if you suspect that the 'maniac' doesn't have much of a hand, there may be someone else behind you who does, and you could easily get trapped on a second-best holding. *Card Player* columnist and author Bob Ciaffone goes so far as to call the seat to the immediate left of such a bulldozer, the 'death seat' – the one place to be avoided in a hold'em game.

Short-Handed Play

At brick and mortar cardrooms short-handed (i.e. six players or fewer) games are generally quite unpopular. The nature of poker is such that each game requires a table and a dealer whether there are four players or ten, so from the cardroom's point of view, full games are a far more economically viable option. Furthermore, many players are uncomfortable playing in short-handed games, which require that they make adjustments to their play, since the standard full 10-player ring game tactics are usually unprofitable in this instance. Indeed, some players try to avoid playing short-handed at all, if possible, either taking a break or leaving the game altogether when numbers run short, whereas those players who do prefer short-handed games are often able to play for only a brief while before the game either fills up or breaks up altogether.

However, as a result of online poker a new breed of player has emerged – the short-handed specialist. These players focus on the special five- and six-player (and even heads-up) tables that most sites offer as an alternative to normal ring games. Unlike brick and mortar cardrooms, online sites are generally more than happy to accommodate these short-handed tables, since of course they do not have to pay a dealer or take up valuable floor space with such games. Furthermore, the fast-paced nature of these games is ideal for the cardroom from a rake standpoint.

The main attraction of online short-handed games from the player's point of view is obvious: such games are dealt at a much quicker rate than a normal ring game (typically well over 100 hands per hour for hold'em), so if you are the best player at the table, your advantage will be greatly enhanced. In addition, the quite different nature of the short-handed game (in particular, the increased importance of attacking and defending the blinds since, with the blinds coming around so quickly, you cannot afford simply to wait for premium hands) lends itself more to a looser, more aggressive 'action' style of play, which is particularly suited to those players who don't enjoy having to wait patiently for a good hand. Furthermore, if you are able to identify a desirable opponent, you are that much more likely to be able to benefit from their bad play, whereas in a full game other players may reap the rewards rather than you.

Typically the maximum rake for a typical six-handed game is capped at $2 compared to the usual $3 for a full 10-player ring game, despite the fact that the average pot size is often not that much smaller, since short-handed play generally has more raising and re-raising than full ring play. Set against this, of course, each individual player will be winning a greater percentage of pots than they would in a full game, and will therefore be obliged to pay the rake far more often (although in short-handed games more hands are decided pre-flop, without a rake being charged). Certainly, if you prefer heads-up play, it is important to choose your site carefully, since heads-up rakes can vary tremendously, but in general if you have good control over your oppo-

opponents you should be able to beat the rake in a normal short-handed game.

Rather than focusing on five- or six-player tables *per se*, one strategy that short-handed experts sometimes use is to search out full 10-player ring games that are either just breaking up or just getting underway. This way they are able to compete advantageously against full ring game specialists in a short-handed game, rather than merely against other short-handed specialists.

Whether you are someone who heads straight to the short-handed games, or immediately leaves a game when it is reduced to six players or fewer, is largely a matter of taste. If your playing style leans towards waiting patiently for good opportunities (using better hand selection strategy than most of your opponents), then you will probably be best suited to normal ring games, but if you enjoy the cut-and-thrust of a poker game, in which bluff meets counter-bluff and bet meets check-raise bluff, then online short-handed games may prove to be your forte.

Deciding how long to play for

The wonderful thing about online poker is that the action never stops – and the terrible thing about online poker is that the action never stops!

In a recent article at casino.com, journalist Andrew Glazer stated that 'the (second-) biggest mistake you can make playing poker online' is to play when you know you only have time for a short (10-20) minute session. (Incidentally, in case you are wondering what he put forward as his choice of biggest mistake – it is playing at a cardroom where there is a very real chance that you won't get paid whether you win or not.) Glazer believes that short sessions should be avoided if possible, since when you are up against the clock you are liable to flout one of the basic poker principles: 'Don't play too many hands.' Although you could of course run into a sequence of great starting hands, it is more likely that you will receive a string of junk hands that you would normally dump without a second thought, but instead you end up playing some of them just to get some action out of your short time online. In all likelihood you will lose money with these hands, but as Glazer astutely points out, it could be even worse in the long run if you were to win with them, since this may encourage you to pick up bad habits and play even more of these junk hands in future.

Of course, it can be just as damaging to play for too long. Once the weaker players have left the game, you become too tired to play a winning game, or perhaps you sense that you are starting to go on tilt after a few bad beats, it is important to stop right then, before your bankroll starts to suffer. One thing is for sure, even if you have booked a loss for this particular session, you will have a chance to repair the damage – there will certainly be another suitable online game running somewhere or other the next time you log on to your computer.

The No-Limit Explosion

In May 2003 I made my first trip across the pond to Las Vegas, to coincide with the World Series of Poker. At that time the cash games at the Horseshoe (apart from some fairly big pot-limit Omaha games) were almost exclusively limit. There were usually one or two $1/$2 blinds no-limit hold'em games going, but that was it. If you wanted to play no-limit you either had to play in that game or stump up the buy-in for a tournament. And not only was that $1/$2 game the only no-limit game being spread at the Horseshoe, incredibly enough it was the only no-limit cash game in the whole of Vegas! Contrast that to Vegas in 2005, where there are no-limit games in every cardroom, some of them with blinds of $10/$20 or more!

The trend towards no-limit cash games has been reflected in online cardrooms as well. Every online poker room nowadays has no-limit games running 24/7, and some have games with blinds as high as $25/$50 peak times. Inspired both by Chris Moneymaker's rags to riches victory in the 2003 World Series of Poker, and by the World Poker Tour TV series, no-limit cash games (and tournaments) are the fastest-growing form of poker. Limit games remain extremely popular, but no-limit is taking a larger and larger share of the pie. Since many of these no-limit players are newcomers to poker, who are prone to bluff too much and call too often, these games are an attractive feeding ground for many online pros. If you yourself are new to poker, then it is advisable to steer clear of no-limit cash games at first. It is safer (and cheaper) to start out in limit cash games, developing your no-limit skills in tournaments until you have found your feet enough to play in no-limit cash games.

Milestone Hand Promotions

From time to time most sites offer cash give-aways for the participants in a milestone hand (for example in December 2002 Paradise Poker awarded $25,000 to the winner and $1,000 to the other players involved in their 250,000,000th hand). Milestone hand promotions tend to draw in a huge number of players hoping to get lucky and win a big prize, with the result that during such promotions the games are typically softer than usual for the regular players at that site.

Although it is impossible to design a system to hit the milestone hand, your chances will naturally be enhanced if you play two (or more) tables at once. Ideally, these should be short-handed tables since then you will receive more hands and therefore more chances to hit. Even more importantly, if you do hit the lucky hand then you will then have a better chance to scoop the winner's prize, since you will have fewer opponents. However, it is worth noting that play money and heads-up games are usually excluded from such promotions.

Working the Lobby

'If I'm going to take a gamble, I want to make sure I have the best of it.'
Puggy Pearson, 1973 WSOP Champion

At the heart of every playing site is the lobby, which provides players with a menu of the games that are currently on offer. Here each game is listed with the table name, stakes, number of players seated in the game, number of players on the waiting list and average pot size (typically based on the last 20 hands). Several sites also offer additional information on the number of players per flop (or fourth street for seven-card stud) and the number of hands played per hour.

If a game in which you wish to participate is currently fully occupied, you will be directed to join a waiting list and then prompted to take a seat once one becomes available. You may choose to use time spent on the waiting list to scout the game, identifying which players are aggressive, which participate in nearly every hand, which may be on tilt etc. If there is more than one game going on at your preferred limit, then it is advisable to join each waiting list individually rather than opt for a 'first available table' option. You then retain the option to pick and choose a table when the time comes, rather than be forced to either take the first available seat or rejoin the waiting list at the back of the queue, should you decide that the table on offer is unsuitable.

Every player has their own views on what constitutes an attractive game for their style of play: some prefer loose games with many players involved in each hand; and others tight games in which they can steal pots with aggressive play. If the site at which you play provides information on the average number of players involved in each pot, then you may like to use it to help you choose the right game for your style. However, as we have stated, it is important to note that the averages provided are typically based on only the last 20 or so hands, depending on the site, and the departure or arrival of a single player can often have a marked effect on the characteristics of a game. Indeed, even a table comprising the same players can sometimes experience a marked shift in dynamics immediately after a big pot has been won and lost.

Many sites also use lobby space to provide a list of the players seated at each table. If you keep notes on your opponents, this information can be invaluable, enabling you to steer away from players whose games you respect and towards those whom you reckon to fare well against. Furthermore, you may be able to identify some players who are playing more than one table at once – at times these players can prove to be ideal opponents, since you may be able to run over them while they are concentrating on the other games they are playing. Multi-table players normally play in quite straightforward fashion, so you should respect their raises and at the same time look to exploit their vulnerability to a well-timed bluff.

Once you are playing, you should still check back to the lobby periodically to see what new opportunities are on offer. A new game may have started at a limit you prefer, another game may now be populated by players you like to compete against, or maybe the game you are playing in has gone completely flat and simply any other game would be a better bet!

The lobby is an important resource in the armoury of a winning player – work it!

Managing an Online Bankroll

'What is the point of playing poker? To win enough money to be able to continue playing poker!' – Poker adage

Chips Please!

Having selected a game and found a seat, there is one further question that needs to be addressed before starting play – how many chips should you purchase at the start of a session? Typically, when you take a seat you will be prompted to buy-in for a certain amount, e.g. $80 for $2/$4 hold'em, $200 for $5/$10, $800 for $20/$40 etc. These figures are perfectly reasonable for a single session at the respective limits. However, there is certainly an argument for buying-in for a little more than these amounts, since if you experience a bad run at the start of a session, you are less likely to be marked down as a target by the other players – bigger stacks do receive more respect. A buy-in of 20 or 30 big bets is certainly a perfectly acceptable figure when you first sit down. Players who sit down with 10 big bets or fewer immediately draw attention to themselves as perhaps either being inadequately bankrolled or taking a shot at a bigger game than they are used to, perhaps playing with 'scared' money. On rare occasions a player will manage to convert a $50 buy-in at a $5/$10 game into several hundred dollars, but far more often they will quickly run out of funds and be forced to re-buy or leave the table.

The issue of 'money management' is a somewhat controversial one in poker literature. Some players advocate the adoption of a single-session 'stop-loss' policy, whereby if you lose a certain predetermined amount you should immediately quit playing, whereas others argue that you should stay in the game until you are no longer favoured to be making money, regardless of whether you are winning or losing at that particular point.

Until you become an experienced online player, it is certainly worth considering adopting Annie Duke's '30-bet rule', limiting single-session losses to 30 big bets. In an article published at Ultimate-Bet.com, she argues that 'unless you are able to accurately judge how you play compared to others, loss-limiting with the 30-bet rule effectively stops you from dumping off large sums of money in games you may not be able to beat.' Furthermore, it prevents additional losses that may be incurred by being identified as a target by the other players in the game, or possibly either playing too softly or going on tilt: 'By limiting your losses to 30 big bets, you are effectively *minimising* the time you spend playing with a poor table image, playing passively, or steaming at the table, and *maximising* the amount of time you spend playing your A-game,' she adds.

Although $800 may be a sufficient sum for a single session of $20/$40, it is just that – a bankroll for a single session. To allow for the vagaries of chance, a minimum online poker bankroll of $4,000 would probably be required to compete in this game on a regular basis. Indeed, many experts recommend that your total bankroll should ideally be of the order of 300 big bets (i.e. $12,000 or more in this instance), although naturally the higher your hourly earnings rate, the fewer big bets you will require in your bankroll.

If you play only for fun, risking small amounts in micro- or low-limit games with no real aspirations of developing into a higher stakes player, then your bankroll requirement is simply what spare cash you have available and are prepared to put at risk. After all, many people spend thousands of dollars each year on other recreational pursuits such as golf, tennis and skiing, and they do not expect to make a profit from these activities. By the same token, there is of course nothing wrong with playing online poker purely as a hobby rather than as a means of earning money, just so long as you enjoy it and have the spare discretionary income to finance any losses.

Having said that, many people do naturally aspire to be winning players at the higher levels, perhaps one day competing in the big $40/$80 hold'em game at Paradise Poker or the $30/$60 game at PartyPoker. In that case, the following table may be useful. It contains some very rough guidelines which may be helpful in determining your total online bankroll requirements for the standard hold'em limits, together with a suggestion of when you might seriously wish to consider moving up to the next limit, assuming that you have not done so already. It is formulated on the popular theory that you should aim to maintain a bankroll of around 300 big bets at the limit at which you play, gradually moving up in limit as your bankroll increases and you become a proven long-term winner (averaging at least one big bet per hour over the course of at least 100 hours' play) at each succeeding limit.

If you are unable to win at least one big bet an hour in the long run then 300 big bets is insufficient to guard against the going broke, and you would be well advised to play at a lower limit. Furthermore, as Mike Caro has pointed out, the larger your bankroll, the more you should seek to protect it. There is therefore a strong argument for maintaining a larger proportional bankroll as you move up through the limits and your risk-exposure increases.

Game	Bare Minimum	Recommended	Move Up
$0.50/$1 Hold'em	$100	$300	$600
$1/$2 Hold'em	$200	$600	$1,200
$2/$4 Hold'em	$400	$1,200	$1,800
$3/$6 Hold'em	$600	$1,800	$3,000
$5/$10 Hold'em	$1,000	$3,000	$4,800
$8/$16 Hold'em	$1,600	$4,800	$6,000
$10/$20 Hold'em	$2,000	$6,000	$9,000
$15/$30 Hold'em	$3,000	$9,000	$12,000
$20/$40 Hold'em	$4,000	$12,000	$18,000
$30/$60 Hold'em	$6,000	$18,000	$24,000
$40/$80 Hold'em	$8,000	$24,000	N/A

These figures could perhaps be doubled if you are playing exclusively heads-up, where the swings can be up to twice as great (that is, unless you are a truly exceptional heads-up player). However, if you are an Omaha hi/lo rather than hold'em player, a bankroll of 100 rather than 300 big bets might be sufficient for a winning player, since the variance in split games such as Omaha hi/lo is so much lower. (Incidentally, the ante and bring-in structure of online seven-card stud is so variable that it does not lend itself to this kind of linear analysis. For example, the $3/$6 game at PartyPoker and $6/$12 game at Poker-Stars both have the same $0.50 ante structure.)

One problem which many players run into eventually is that, having worked their way up through the limits, gradually building up their bankroll, they then experience a really bad run. At this point it would probably be most prudent for them to drop down in limit in order to replenish their bankroll (and perhaps restore some lost confidence). However, this kind of decision is problematic for many players, since their ego won't let them take what they perceive as a backwards step.

It is also important to remember that losing players actually require a bankroll that is sufficient to finance their losses over a lifetime – the only useful recommendation for such players is to work at their game and become a winning player; bankroll requirements are clearly redundant in this instance.

Whatever the size of your bankroll, it is inadvisable to keep large sums of cash with a single online poker site, unless that amount is required to finance your regular play. There have been instances in the past (such as Pokerspot, as we saw earlier in the book) where sites have gone out of business, leaving a trail of unhappy depositors in their wake, and there is always the possibility that it could happen again. When in doubt – cash out!

If you are used to playing in live-action games, it is worth remembering that in an online game at the same limit your hourly swings will inevitably be much greater, due to the many more hands that you will be dealt every hour – you may therefore find yourself effectively playing 'higher' than you would ordinarily be comfortable with. Whether you are playing in high stakes games or at micro-limits, there is one golden rule to bear in mind – never gamble with money that you cannot afford to lose. Please gamble responsibly.

Online Tells

'In the online game, everyone has the perfect poker face.' Adam Letalik

Whereas in a live-action game, it is sometimes possible to pick up useful visual clues to help ascertain whether an opponent is strong or not, in the online game this element of the game is much less significant. Of course, in online play, just as in live-action games, it is possible to deduce some information about your opponents from their betting patterns, but online tells play a relatively small role overall. In this section we shall discuss the role of online tells – those tells which are unique to the online game.

Telling by Time

It is often argued that the amount of time that an opponent spends on a decision can indicate whether or not he is holding a good hand; hesitation before betting often being used to feign weakness and rapid bets made to try and muscle the pot, or, as Mike Caro puts it, 'weak means strong' and 'strong means weak'.

On the flop, a very quick call often suggest a drawing hand (typically a flush draw), whereas a quick raise often represents top pair with a decent kicker (or an overpair). A very slow call will often mean a mediocre hand (one which the player was seriously considering folding). It is always very unpleasant when someone first checks slowly and then check-raises immediately after you have bet, thereby representing a very strong hand, which is most likely what they are holding.

In general, if the first player makes a very fast bet after everyone has checked on the previous round then this may indicate a bluff to try and pick up this 'orphan' pot, whereas if that player pauses unduly before carrying out a bet (or everyone checks and the last player pauses before betting) then this may suggest that he has a very strong hand and is trying to induce calls through his apparent hesitation (which is sometimes known as the 'stall-bluff').

Players who take a long time over all of their decisions are usually either very new to the game, suffering from a poor Internet connection or playing multiple tables (or otherwise distracted). If you are familiar with the player and identify distraction as the cause, then they are a prime candidate for a well-timed bluff.

Here is a summary of these timing tells:

Pre-flop:

Instant 'auto-raise': High pair or big ace

Lots of instant folds: Tight player

Post-flop:

Quick raise: Probable good made hand

Slow check: Probable weak hand *except:*

Slow check followed by quick check-raise: Probable very big hand

Instant check: Likely very weak hand

Quick bet: May be trying to act strong

Slow bet (or raise): May be trying to act weak

Quick call: Likely drawing hand

Slow call: Marginal hand

Of course, these online tells cannot be applied across the board for all opponents (and they can easily be reversed by sophisticated opponents in any case). Some players will pause to calculate whether they have a reasonable chance of getting away with a bluff, whereas others will act slowly to pretend that they have a hand, in the hope of discouraging you from betting into them on the next round, and thereby gaining a free card. Slow action may also be completely neutral – it may simply be that your opponent was thinking about a decision at another table or was otherwise distracted, or indeed that either you or your opponent is experiencing a lag in their Internet connection (although usually connection problems are ongoing, so you may be able to ascertain whether the delay is likely to be connection-related or not).

A tell is only meaningful if it involves a deviation from your opponent's normal behaviour. If you do spot a tell on your opponent, then it is important to make a note of it, in case you run into a similar situation with him in the future.

In principle, you should spend as much time on each decision as you need, varying the time you spend on your decisions if you feel you are becoming too predictable or alternatively seeking to take exactly the same amount of time before each action, regardless of whether you are betting a big hand or a marginal one. Indeed, if you stop to think too often you may take some of the fun element out of the game for the other players, encouraging them either to go elsewhere to gamble or to concentrate harder on their own decisions! Some of the best online games are those in which everyone else is enjoying themselves, chatting to one another, playing quickly and not paying a great deal of attention to the real action on the table.

Giving the Game away in Advance

Advance-action check-boxes are now a standard feature of all online poker sites. Overall they are a great enhancement, speeding up the game and allowing players the liberty to, say, fold before time to go and put the kettle on, rather than having to wait and then fold only when it comes around to their turn. Certainly you should use these boxes to 'auto-post' your blinds, muck your losing hands and fold in the face of a bet when you have absolutely no intention of contesting the pot, since it is in everyone's interests to keep the games running smoothly. However, a degree of caution should be exercised when using some of these check-boxes. First, because the screen selection can sometimes change just as you make your action and you may end up, say, accidentally calling when you meant to check; and second because the observant player can sometimes take advantage of the clues that your use of check-boxes may provide.

For example, let's say you have pocket aces in hold'em before the flop. You decide to raise and click the advance box 'raise any'. The action comes to you and you end up instantly re-raising after a player directly to your right has just raised. This instantaneous action may tip off the whole table to the fact that you have a big pocket pair, and could have a negative effect on your business. Likewise if you bet and someone raises instantaneously behind you, then they quite possibly have a big hand. Paradoxically, some players try to simulate use of the 'raise any' box by acting almost instantaneously when they are or on or next to the button and no-one else has yet entered the pot, hoping to steal the blinds by persuading the remaining players that they would have raised regardless. Late position players who hesitate before opening the betting with a raise (either through actual or feigned weakness) are in general that much more likely to be called or challenged by a three-bet from one of the remaining players.

An even more common way in which using check-boxes can provide a tell is the advance-action 'check' or 'check-fold' box. Many players use these boxes when the flop misses them altogether and they are waiting for an early position player to act. However, this instant action is very likely to tip off a late position player that you have nothing and as a result he may elect to bet, whereas otherwise he might have checked (fearing a check-raise from you) and thereby allowed you a potentially valuable free card. And of course, in the opposite scenario, if you check in early position and the other players all immediately check behind you, there is a good chance that they have nothing and you may be able to run a bluff if a blank comes on the next street. If you do run across a player who habitually uses the 'check' or 'check-fold' boxes, it is well worth making a note of their name. Next time you come across them just sit to their left and get ready to steal!

Even when you use the 'fold' advance-action box regularly to fold pre-flop, you may be giving away information to your opponents. The fact that you are folding instantly in many situations, regardless of the action in the hand so far, will tip off an observant player to the fact that you are playing very tightly. He may then start raising your blinds with any two cards and putting you under pressure.

Generally, it is recommended that you keep you have away from your mouse until it is your turn to act. This has several advantages:

♠ You won't give away any information by using the advance-action boxes.

♠ You won't accidentally click on 'call' rather than 'check' if the screen changes just before you act.

♠ You won't be surfing the Internet or writing e-mails while you are playing!

What's in a Name?

Can you judge players by their online handles? Is Mad Dog 666 likely to be a 'maniac', betting every hand to the river in a wild flurry of action? And is Jam Doughnut a 'weak-tight' player, whom you can easily push off a hand? And can you judge a player by the picture they choose to represent themselves with at PokerStars, for example?

Rather than focusing on the names or images people give themselves, you should concentrate on closely observing their play. After 10 or 15 minutes, you should be able to form a reliable impression of what style of player they are from the way they play their cards, rather than whether or not they have a macho name or picture. Also watch out for players with female names – some of them are men in disguise, hoping that you are either going to take it easy on them, bluff into them or chat them up! Conversely, some women prefer not to give any indication of their gender, either because they do not want to give their opponents any unnecessary information, or simply to avoid attracting male attention.

Some players use the same handle at every site they play, whereas others prefer to use a different handle at each site. It is certainly an advantage to have multiple handles if you fear that your opponents are taking notes on you, since they won't recognise you when you are playing at a different site.

Other Tells

You can often pick up how good a player is purely by whether they use the chat box or not. In general, good players do not waste their time chatting at length to their opponents (or moaning about bad beats). Excessive chatting by an opponent is often a good indicator that they are a weak player, particularly if they are moaning about the play of others at the table.

It is often possible to gain an idea about an opponent's style before they have even received their first hand. If they post a blind in early or middle position (rather than waiting for the big blind) then they are usually impatient to get the action underway – you can expect plenty of loose action from such an early poster. Someone who has been routinely auto-posting blinds but then stops doing so may be about to leave the game, and thus could be less inclined to gamble in a marginal situation.

Sometimes you can draw information about a player from the size of their buy-in. Players who buy-in for the minimum allowed are typically playing with 'scared' money, and are good candidates to go broke. Conversely, good, experienced players often buy-in for an amount larger than the 'recommended' table buy-in, because they know that they will experience big swings (and may want to use their stack size to intimidate their opponents).

Another tell applies only to pot-limit and no-limit games. Players sometimes bet very strange amounts purely to make their bets look larger than they really are. In that case, most probably the player does not want you to call (or even raise!).

Showing Cards

Many players make a habit of proudly showing off their winning hands even when they don't need to. Although this practice is not strictly a tell, it does provide you with free information on how they play and should be encouraged wherever possible. Some players like to make a comment like 'nh' (nice hand) or 'yes, you had me beaten there' to reinforce this behaviour, inducing the show-off to keep displaying their winning hands for free. Conversely, there are also players who often show their hands when they have just endured a bad beat. Apart from providing the same information on their playing style, this can also sometimes indicate that they are feeling sorry for themselves and may be about to go on tilt.

By the same token, it is undesirable for you to provide your opponents with free information about the cards you are playing, unless you have an ulterior motive. For example, you may sometimes wish to reveal that you had a big hand when you originally opened the betting with a late position raise, in order to set up an out-and-out steal in a similar situation somewhere down the line.

Taking Notes

Most sites now offer the facility to take notes on other players, which are then stored on your computer and can be retrieved the next time you run into them at the tables. You can write whatever you like in these private notes – what kinds of hands the player is showing down, what their pre-flop raising (and calling) standards are like, whether they are aggressive or passive, tight or loose, whether or not they always defend their blinds, whether or not they always launch an attack on other people's blinds when they are first in from late position, whether or not they are prone to going on tilt after a bad beat, whether or not they are capable of running big bluffs etc.

When an unfamiliar new player enters a hold'em game it is often worth noting whether they wait for the big blind (or let it pass and then post next to the button) or post at the first available opportunity, even if they are shortly due for the big blind anyhow. In the latter instance, it may be that they are an 'action' player, impatient to start gambling.

If you do not wish to take detailed notes, it is still worth recording who the big winners and losers were at the table, so that over time you can develop a feel for who the best and worst players are at the limit you play, and can subsequently select your opponents accordingly.

For Paradise Poker, PokerStars and PartyPoker, you can actually edit your notes when you are not actually online – simply open up the 'Notes' text file in the local directory in which your online site is stored and all your data should be there. It may be as well to take a backup copy of this file before you make any changes, so that you don't lose it if something goes wrong. Of course, if you change computers this text file can be copied across to your new machine to save you having to start from scratch all over again. (N.B. At Paradise Poker the file is called 'Player Notes' rather than 'Notes'.)

Online note-taking facilities are not available at every site (and are not portable from site to site), so some players prefer to store their notes either handwritten in a notebook, or on their PC in a word-processing document or spreadsheet. Of course, the latter approach has the important advantage that it is easier to store and sort your notes. If you wish to keep notes in this format then you may choose to layout your notes in the following columns:

♠ The player's name.

♠ The player's location (most sites provide this information nowadays).

♠ The date.

♠ The type of game and limit at which you encountered the player.

♠ An approximate rating for that player (on a scale of 1-5 or 1-10).

♠ An indication of their general starting hand requirements and pre-flop style – Loose? Tight? Passive? Aggressive? (You could even add specific examples to help jog your memory.) What kinds of hands did they steal and defend blinds with?

♠ An indication of their post-flop style of play. What kinds of hands did they bet or raise? Top pair with good kicker? Top pair with bad kicker? Bottom pair? Flush/straight draws? Outright bluffs?

♠ Any other points of interest. For example: Did they vary their play? Did they go on tilt after a bad beat? Did they trap with very big hands? Did they reveal anything about their playing style in any chat messages? Were they playing at more than one table? Do they regularly play at a different limit to today's game? etc.

It is sometimes argued that unless you are playing at limits of, say, $10/$20 or above, note-taking can hardly be worthwhile, since below that limit there are so many players that you will not run into them often enough to justify the time invested. However, others believe that note-taking is an important skill which you should constantly try to develop as you progress through the limits. Furthermore, it will encourage you to focus properly on your opponents' play, whereas otherwise your attention might be diverted away from the game. Even at lower limits, you will find that from time to time your notes on another player will help steer you towards the right path in a tricky situation. If nothing else you may wish to keep a notepad by your PC listing the best players whom you have faced; and the ones whom you figure might form part of your 'dream-team' of potential opponents!

If you play online stud (but cannot always remember the upcards perfectly) then you may wish to consider keeping a sheaf of photocopied sheets by your computer, each of which contains (allowing for some blank space between them so that you do not get muddled between one hand and the next), say, 12 copies of the following:

Ad	Ah	Ac	As
Kd	Kh	Kc	Ks
Qd	Qh	Qc	Qs
Jd	Jh	Jc	Js
Td	Th	Tc	Ts
9d	9h	9c	9s
8d	8h	8c	8s
7d	7h	7c	7s
6d	6h	6c	6s
5d	5h	5c	5s
4d	4h	4c	4s
3d	3h	3c	3s
2d	2h	2c	2s

Starting a new list for each new hand, you can simply cross off the up-cards as they are dealt, and can thereby retain the option of referring back to the list should you forget any of the folded upcards as the hand develops.

At the end of each session you should also strongly consider taking notes on yourself! Typically this might take the form of a word-processing or spreadsheet document and include the following information:

♠ The date

♠ The length of the playing session (measured either in minutes, hands played or both).

♠ The site at which you played (assuming that you have accounts at two or more sites).

♠ The form in which the game was played (assuming that you play more than one form of poker).

♠ The limit at which the game was played (or the buy-in level in the case of a tournament).

♠ The amount won or lost.

You may also like to keep a note of how many flops you saw, the percentage of games you won and other such statistics, if this information is provided by the site at which you play. Once you have built up a series of such records, you should be able to develop a good feel for the type of games in which you fare best, which will greatly assist your game selection in future.

In a recent edition of *Online Poker News*, Andrew Glazer even recommended taking notes on specific plays you make that save or lose you money, and adding these up at the end of the session to see what these plays have earned or cost you. That way, if you keep making the same mistakes from one session to the next, the cost of these should be plain to see!

Another important means whereby you can analyse your own play is through hand histories, to which we now turn.

Hand Histories and Statistics

Nowadays, hand histories are a standard feature of online poker sites.

These are sometimes available in an 'instant' format and sometimes supplied by e-mail (and often both). Each method has pluses and minuses. If you are able to view your hand histories instantly, then you can review them straight after a hand, rather than having to wait for an e-mail, but on the other hand the e-mail method has the advantage that the hand histories are automatically stored in your inbox and can be referred to days or even months later. Furthermore, at some sites these e-mails come in a standard format that can be read into a program such as Poker Tracker or PokerStat, which may then reveal valuable insights into both your own play and that of your opponents.

Programs like Poker Tracker collect and combine your hand histories into a database, and then allow you to run a wide range of database queries. It will tell you what percentage of flops you are seeing, how you fare with each pair of hold'em pocket cards, how often you raise before the flop or give up your blinds uncontested etc. – and also provides you with the same information for each of your opponents! Indeed, you can even create a 'Game Time' table, which provides the key information on all of your opponents, viewable at a glance.

If you are fortunate enough to have a coach, then hand histories are an extremely helpful basis for analysis and discussion; and you could always write up and post any of your particularly interesting hand histories on a poker newsgroup or forum to invite comments and suggestions. Just remember to provide as much information as possible both about the hand, and the dynamics of the table at that particular time, so that the exact situation you were in can be recreated as accurately as possible. And it would probably be as well to prepare yourself for some blunt criticism from the 'experts'!

Whether you plan to ask for feedback on your hands or not, it is still important to review the hand histories of the key hands that you played in each session. Did you play well or could you have saved or gained some extra bets? Did your opponents make mistakes or did they pull off any clever plays that you might be able to use yourself at a later date? Once you have reviewed and annotated your key hands, you might like to consider placing them in a file to which you can refer back at a later date. Having amassed a number of these hands, you may then be able to identify recurring positive or negative features of your play, which will enable you to improve your future results.

What were they calling with?

One unique feature of hand histories at some (but not all) sites is that they reveal the pocket cards of players who called at the showdown, even if they failed to win the pot. At a brick and mortar cardroom, the caller on the end is almost always allowed to muck losing hands without showing their cards, but at PokerStars, for example, this valuable information is available instantly.

Consider the following scenario: Playing at your favourite site, you have a good hand, so you bet and get called all the way to the river. You show down your good hand, it holds up, and your opponent mucks. For once, you haven't been suffered a bad beat on the end – wonder of wonders!

A little while later, the same thing happens. You get called down and again you win (winning two showdowns in a row – it really is your lucky day!) and your opponent mucks. When the euphoria of winning two showdowns in a row subsides, you start to wonder if your opponent may be a calling station and not the type of player against whom you might, for example, want to try and run a bluff.

But how can you be sure? Maybe he also had a good hand, was making legitimate calls and just got a little unlucky with a lower kicker. Well, check the hand history. Even if your opponent mucks at the showdown, his hand is normally revealed if he has called on the river. You can therefore find out what he was doing in the hand and get a handle on what kind of a player he is. Note that this also applies even if you are not involved in the showdown yourself – you can still see what the other players involved in the showdown were going to war with. This difference between online and offline play can provide valuable insights into your opponents' play and you should not shy away from taking advantage of it.

Statistics

Many sites (for example Paradise Poker and PokerStars) currently offer their users a set of statistics on their play. Whilst these are nothing like as comprehensive as those provided by a dedicated online poker tracking program such as Poker Tracker, they can still provide you with some useful information. For example, Paradise Poker provides a pop-up box which logs your statistics for each session and displays the following information in percentages:

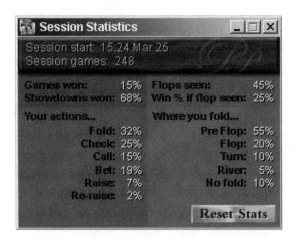

Games won – This is not really a particularly useful statistic, since the purpose of playing poker is not to win as many hands as possible but to win money! Many players with a high 'games won' percentage will lose money overall, but will win a high number of hands purely due to the fact that they contest more pots to the river than they should. Furthermore, when you win a split pot it is counted in the statistics as a full win, which slightly inflates the games won percentage.

Showdowns won – This statistic provides a more practical indication of your play, since it reveals how often you display the winning hand at the river. If your long-run 'showdowns won' percentage is considerably below 45% (for full 10-player hold'em ring games) then you may be seeing too many hands through to the river and may wish to re-evaluate your play accordingly. For tight players a long-run 'showdowns won' percentage of 55%-60% should be perfectly achievable. However, the 'showdowns won' figure should be used with some caution – if you would have folded to a bet on the end but it was checked down instead, then this goes down as a showdown lost.

Flops seen – This is the most useful statistic. There are no hard and fast rules on what percentage of flops you should be seeing, since in any single session your percentage will be largely dependent on how aggressively your opponents are playing. Indeed, a handful of extra free or cheap plays from the blinds can totally distort your overall percentage. The best way to gauge how loosely you are playing at any point in time, is to compare your own 'flops seen' percentage with that of the table as a whole – if you are above average then you may possibly be seeing too many flops.

As for the long run, if your 'flops seen' percentage (for full hold'em 10-player ring games) is consistently higher than 30%, then you may wish to consider whether you are playing too loosely – many experts would argue that it should be as low as 18-25% in the long run. (Incidentally, PokerStars breaks the 'flops seen' figure down into 'small blind', 'big blind' and 'other positions', which is quite informative if you wish to analyse whether you are contesting too few or too many hands from the blinds.)

Win % if flop seen (or fourth street for stud) – This statistic is very closely correlated to the preceding one. A long-run figure of less than 20% may indicate that you are perhaps seeing too many flops with sub-standard hands.

Your actions – These percentages should give you an indication of how passively or aggressively you are playing, and will vary greatly from player to player depending on individual styles of play. As a rough guide, if your call percentage is significantly larger than the sum of your bet, raise and reraise percentages combined, then you may wish to consider whether you are playing too passively.

Where you fold – Again, these figures will depend greatly on your style of play, but they may provide you with an indication of whether you are folding too much or too little.

Naturally, these statistics only become meaningful with a representative sample size. With only 50 or fewer hands they offer only a very brief snapshot of play, and should not be considered at all reliable, but as you play more and more hands they will provide a much more useful indication of your play. Paradise Poker does offer the facility to run on these statistics from one session to the next (rather than resetting them from zero at the beginning of each new session), and by the time you have accumulated statistics on 1,000 or more games, they should offer quite a good reflection of your playing style. (In order to preserve your stats for the next session, simply right-click on the palm tree in the top left of the stats box and select 'Preserve stats next session'; using the same basic procedure you may also choose to save your stats to disk or paste them to your clipboard.)

Cybertilt and running bad

'My edge over the typical player when we are both running good is not nearly as great as when we are both running bad.' Dan Harrington – 1995 WSOP Champion

From time to time even the most dispassionate player may lose his calm, disciplined approach to the game and instead start making decisions that are heavily guided by his emotions, in other words, go on tilt like a pinball machine. Some players with an extensive knowledge of poker fail to make the most of their talent, largely because they are unable to play their best game consistently – too often they allow their emotions to take over. Probably the most common scenario for tilt to manifest itself occurs when a player has just endured a bad beat (or series of bad beats) and succumbs to the natural urge to try and get even as quickly as possible, but it could just be that the player is enduring a poor session overall and suffering a deterioration in his play as a result.

With the enhanced speed of online play, relative to live play, everything is compounded and it is even easier to go on tilt – hand after hand is dealt in quick succession, and there is no time to calm down, take stock, properly rationalise the situation and regroup. In the online game your chips are only a number on the screen, and the fact that these 'cyberchips' have no physical presence makes it easier to lose sight of the fact that they represent real money and should not be treated lightly. Furthermore, in a live-action game, social convention dictates that you should not blow off steam in public, whereas online there are no constraints to prevent you from openly losing your temper and steaming your way through your bankroll. The risk of going on tilt is further magnified if you are playing two or more tables at once, where money can be won (or in this case lost) twice as fast.

One problem which players often face when they are enduring a losing session, is that the other players in the game see them struggling and try to take advantage of this, perhaps by playing draws more aggressively against them or running more bluffs. Not only does the player now have to face the emotional setback of a losing session, but also the reality that other players are now queuing up to take shots at him, forcing him to deal with a series of difficult decisions. Apart from the obvious course of action – to leave the table – one alternative way of avoiding this nightmare scenario is to discretely buy more chips, thereby disguising the fact that you are actually losing. As long as you retain broadly the same amount of chips throughout a game, most players won't notice whether you are winning or losing, and therefore won't play any differently against you. Of course, the very worst thing you can do when you are losing is to start criticising the other players for their play through chat messages – this will merely alert them to the fact that you may be on tilt and encourage them to play even better against you! Likewise, if you see someone else berating the other players through the chat box, then this may present a good opportunity since he could be about to go tilt and steam away some chips.

The nature of poker is such that from time to time every player will experience a large financial reverse, either from a disastrous single session or a series of losing sessions. Even top players can experience long sequences of poor results (although this does not mean that if you achieve bad results you must be a top player!). Different players have different ways of dealing with such setbacks: some go to watch the high-limit heads-up games at UltimateBet, where the thousands of dollars that can be won and lost on every hand make their losses seem small by comparison; others take a break for a few days or spend some time reviewing their play and reading books; others practise relaxation techniques to try to restore their equilibrium; others try out a different site or switch to a different form of poker for a while; and others drop down in limit or try to log a few short winning sessions to restore their confidence. Any of these methods is likely to be preferable to playing on tilt, making plays that you know are incorrect in a vain attempt to get even, in a game that has long since turned sour. It is not enough to be a good player; you must also play well on a consistent basis.

Online Chat

'You don't lose players when you bar an abusive player, you gain players.' Johnny Moss, poker legend

Nowadays every major poker site provides the facility for players to chat with one another. Most players enjoy making conversation from time to time, since it helps reduce the isolation of playing online, adding a social element to the game that online poker would otherwise lack. Sometimes players use the chat boxes to praise or berate opponents, sometimes to help iron out any issues that may have arisen at the table, and other times just to catch up with friends whom they have met through the cardroom. Of course, it is forbidden for anyone to use the chat function to even hint at what their hole cards are or advise other players on how they should play a hand that is in progress!

Very often players use common abbreviations when they are chatting to save typing time, the most common of which are:

bb – *big blind*
brb – *be right back*
g1 – *good one*
gc – *good cards (or good call)*
gg – *good game*
gh – *good hand*
gl – *good luck*
lol – *laughing out loud*
n1 – *nice one*
nc – *nice cards (or nice catch)*
nh – *nice hand*
np – *no problem*

rofl – *rolling on the floor laughing*
sb – *small blind*
tx – *thanks*
ty – *thank you*
tyvm – *thank you very much*
vnh – *very nice hand*
wd – *well done*
wp – *well played*
yw – *you're welcome*
zzzzzzz – *hurry up, I'm falling asleep over here!*

It has already been mentioned that some of the best opportunities in online play arise when all the other players at the table are chatting to one another, enjoying the camaraderie of the game instead of focusing properly on the game itself. If everyone is relaxed and having a good time, it is much more likely that the game will be played in the kind of gambling spirit that you are looking for in a game – everyone playing looser than they normally would and the bad players staying at the table even if they are losing money. If you are fortunate enough to find yourself at such a table, then it is not at all in your interests to jeopardise the spirit of the game – if you don't wish to participate in the banter yourself, that's fine, but if you want everyone to keep playing in the same fashion, then it is better to hold your peace rather than to say anything that may cause a change in the atmosphere of the game.

By the same token, you should avoid criticising another player for playing a hand badly – by embarrassing another player in public you will either cause them to leave with their bankroll still intact, or more likely encourage them to pay more attention to the game, tightening up, playing better and perhaps learning some valuable lessons for the future. As the saying goes 'Don't tap on the glass!'

It is sometimes argued that the best way to part a bad player from their money is to try and set them on tilt by verbally attacking them. However, this is a somewhat short-sighted strategy – if you come across a player who really is that clueless, they are probably easy to beat anyhow. Surely you want them in your game on a regular basis? Why spoil their gambling experience and cause them to go elsewhere in future?

Occasionally you will have the misfortune to find yourself at a table where a player is ranting and raving, and possibly even being extremely abusive to other players. Invariably that player is on tilt, steaming through their bankroll. In these circumstances there are three non-exclusive courses of action:

♠ You owe it to yourself (and all the other polite players at the table) to play your best game against the abusive player, helping to relieve him of his bankroll and sending him off with his tail between his legs. Don't get involved in an argument with him and allow his bad behaviour to put you on tilt!

♠ Just as in a brick and mortar cardroom where you can report abuse to the dealer or floorperson, so you can report chat abuse to the online poker room's customer support team, who will often relieve abusive players of their chat privileges for a designated period. If you file a legitimate complaint and the cardroom fails to act, this may tell you everything you need to know about whether or not you should be providing that particular site with your future business.

♠ Finally, you can always switch off the chat feature if you wish, although this is rather an unsatisfactory solution if you like to use the chat yourself or enjoy trying to gain clues about the other players through their chat messages.

It is important to remember that in Internet poker you are completely anonymous. No-one knows anything about you except your online name, and what they may or may not have been able to glean from the way you play your cards. As soon as you start to chat you risk giving away information about yourself, which other players may be able to use in forming strategies to beat you. For example, if you moan about a couple of bad beats, the sharks may identify you as a frustrated and mediocre player, and start regarding you as a target of their upcoming play. Players who mark themselves as potential victims are inevitably likely to be victimised.

If you do enjoy chatting then it might be worth considering using an online handle which sounds approachable – if you use a name such as Andrew73 other players may be more inclined to chat with you than if you call yourself something like hgtmvshmr.

Playing Two or More Tables at once – Twice the Risk or Double the Fun?

One unique feature of online poker is the facility to play two or more online tables at once, either at one site or several different sites. Many experienced players like to take advantage of this opportunity. Indeed, double World Poker Tour winner Erick Lindgren says that early in his career he used to play eight tables at once!

Although multi-table players recognise that they won't be able to play quite so well on two or more tables as they could on a single table, they figure that although they may not earn as much *per table*, their overall *hourly rate* will be improved. For example, a player who is able to win two big bets per hour playing at a single table may choose to play two tables instead. Although it is extremely unlikely that they will now be able to make two big bets per hour *at each table*, they may still very well be able to increase their *overall* hourly rate to two and a half or three big bets. Furthermore, if they are actually able to play more or less as well on two lower-limit tables as they can on one larger-limit table, their overall variance should be lower, thereby reducing the chance of a prolonged downswing in their bankroll. In essence, by playing more than one table you are arriving at the 'long run' faster than you would be otherwise.

Playing more than one table is a good way of avoiding the frustration that can arise when the game is slow or you encounter a long series of unplayable starting hands. By playing two or more tables, you are actually less likely to fall into the trap of playing too many starting hands, since there is enough activity to keep you occupied, and you can avoid getting sucked into playing marginal hands just to combat the tedium of having to fold hand after hand. However, it is important to recognise that if you are only a break-even player when you play at a single table, then you should avoid playing simultaneous tables, since you will most likely become a losing player.

If you do choose to play more than one table, then you should first ensure that the tables are not lined up precisely one on top of the other on your screen, but instead overlap in some way, otherwise you may find yourself accidentally raising on one table when you meant to fold and vice-versa (UltimateBet actually provides an excellent MiniView™ feature, which allows players to play multiple tables with no overlapping whatsoever). You may in fact wish to experiment with adjusting your screen resolution in order to fit two tables at once on your desktop (in Windows go to 'Control Panel', then to 'Display', then to 'Settings' and adjust your screen resolution as required; 1024x768 is probably adequate for most players, depending on the size of your monitor). Some regular multi-table players (myself included!) have even set up their computers with two monitors and a dual monitor graphics card. With this set-up it is easier to focus on multiple games, perhaps even playing four or more tables at once.

Many players dislike playing simultaneously on two tables for the very simple reason that they find it difficult to keep track of the action, and struggle to cope with the constant barrage of betting decisions. One clear disadvantage of playing on more than one table is that you will miss out on witnessing many of the hands in which you are not participating. You may therefore struggle to pick up on the tendencies of your opponents, perhaps failing to spot that one player is a habitual bluffer, or that another has purchased three re-buys and is completely on tilt. If you play in games in which the players are of more or less equal ability, then playing in two games may not have much of a negative effect on your hourly expectation, but if there are one or two players who are of sub-par standard, then playing two tables hampers your chances of identifying those players and picking on their weaknesses. You should also bear in mind that it is much more difficult to make proper, reliable notes on your opponents for future use when you are playing two tables at once.

Furthermore, when playing multiple tables, some of your actions will also inevitably be rushed 'reflex' decisions rather than rationally thought through, which could prove very dangerous unless you have an excellent fundamental understanding of the game in which you are playing. Multi-table players are also almost certainly much more susceptible to allowing their blinds to be stolen or being bluffed, either because they are more likely to use the advance-action boxes and tip their hand, or because they are perhaps focusing on a key hand elsewhere and don't have the time or inclination to work out whether an opponent might be running a bluff. Conversely, if someone whom you know is playing multiple tables at once puts a strong play on you, the chances are that they really do have the goods!

If you are prone to going on tilt, you should probably avoid playing multiple tables – the action is so fast and furious that it is especially hard to keep a rein on your emotions after a couple of bad beats. Playing two stud games at once can also be very problematic – many players struggle to remember the folded upcards on one table, let alone two at once! And trying to cope with several short-handed games at once would also be living a little too close to the edge for most players. Finally, it is rather inadvisable to play a hi/lo game and a hi game at the same time – it is all too easy to mix up the tables and raise with the nut low in the hi game!

Next time you find yourself playing two tables, ask yourself – 'Which is the weaker game and would I be better off dropping the other table and just focusing on that one?' Or to look at it another way, 'If I'm playing one table myself would I prefer that my opponents were all focusing on that table or each playing two or three tables at once?' When you are working the lobby looking for a game, you may wish to pay particular attention to any tables that include several players who are trying to play multiple games at once – they may prove to be good opponents. And if you do decide to play two tables, it is well worth considering dropping down in limit to minimise your risk, for example a $2/$4 player might choose to play two $1/$2 tables, or a $5/$10 player, two $3/$6 tables.

Online Props

A proposition player (or prop) is a player who is paid by the house to start up new games and keep existing games going, while encouraging a friendly atmosphere among the players. Unlike a shill, a prop player plays with and risks his own (and not the house's) money. Prop players have been a feature of many brick and mortar cardrooms for years, and several major online cardrooms do employ (or have employed) props. In particular, it is quite common for new sites to employ props to help generate regular traffic during their launch period. However, not every site uses props – PokerStars and True Poker, for example, have both gone so far as to post unequivocally on public forums that they are not employing props.

An online prop can typically expect to earn something in the region of $12-$15 an hour (and perhaps more if they are prepared to play two tables at once) with their precise income determined by the number of hands they play. In general, props are required to play at the lower range of limits (typically, say, from $2/$4 to $5/10).

For some players, online prop play may be an attractive option, for the following reasons:

♠ Prop players receive payment for doing what they may have been doing anyway (playing online poker).

♠ Prop players can usually choose their own working hours.

♠ Prop players can normally play online as a second 'part-time' job.

However, prop play also has some disadvantages as well:

♠ Prop players risk their own money – if they lose then they not only have no income (apart from their prop pay), but may also find themselves out of a job if their bankroll runs out.

♠ Prop players are obliged to play a certain number of hours at the one site, and therefore do not have the same freedom to employ site selection strategies (at least not during their prop payment hours) as other players.

♠ Prop players have to play at the table to which they are directed by the cardroom, and are therefore unable to employ game selection strategies.

♠ Prop players usually have to move tables at the cardroom's discretion (for example, sometimes having to vacate a table at which they were winning once that table is full, and finding themselves being placed instead at a short-handed table with several known tricky opponents).

♠ Since prop players are typically paid 'per hand', if there is no-one to play against they can't earn any income.

♠ Prop players usually have to play a great deal of short-handed play, since one of their main functions is to start new games. However, many potential candidates for prop play do not enjoy playing short-handed, and the variance for such games is greater than for full ring games, so a larger bankroll is necessary to handle the fluctuations. Furthermore, those props who lack proficiency at short-handed or heads-up play are an open target for specialist short-handed experts to attack in 'hit and run' raids. To offset this, at least in part, props usually earn more when they play short-handed, since they will play many more hands per hour in these games than they would in a full ring game.

It takes a particular kind of player to be successful as a prop – someone who is skilled at (and able to survive the fluctuations of) short-handed play, and also capable of returning a profit despite very limited opportunities for game selection. Although some players do enjoy working as props, most top online professionals prefer to retain their independence (particularly since many professionals would typically be playing higher than $5/$10 in any case).

For some reason, many online players are afraid of props, assuming that they must naturally be very good players, but in fact there is no real reason to fear playing against a prop player any more than you would be wary of any other experienced online player. In fact, it would be counter-productive for cardrooms to employ props who play *outstandingly* well, since such players might win too much money from the other players and actually reduce the number of active players on the site.

It is sometimes argued that cardrooms should reveal the identities of their props, whose play they are in effect subsidising. However, so long as they are playing at their own risk and have no advantages over the other players (other than the fact that they are being paid for the number of hands in which they participate; at most sites props are not even told who the other props are), it is doubtful what real purpose would be served by removing their anonymity.

One very popular method that cardrooms use to generate traffic without using props is to offer deposit bonuses. Typically these bonuses amount to 15%-25% of the deposit amount, but the bonus is only paid when the player has qualified by playing a predetermined number of raked hands. In addition, the cash prizes for some freeroll tournaments are also only released when the player has fulfilled a similar quota of raked hands. Effectively these players are acting as informal props, keeping games occupied in return for their bonuses or prizes, although of course the site does not have the right to tell them at which table they must play.

Software

One of the most fundamental issues for any online business is security – unless clients can trust that the software is providing them with complete security then they will be reluctant to engage in any online transaction, gambling or otherwise. Major online poker sites offer the same protection against hackers that banks do. At PartyPoker, for example, your playing cards, name, address, credit card details, password (and everything else that is transmitted to and from the cardroom) are protected from 'packet-sniffers' by the internationally-accepted industry-standard SSLv3/TLSv1 encryption algorithm system. Furthermore, your own playing cards are sent exclusively to your computer – no-one else has access to your downcards.

Apart from providing customer security, the other main interface requirements of an online poker site are speed, reliability and an intuitive and attractive design. In the early days of online poker, games were often slow, with players experiencing frequent disconnection problems and having to cope with clunky, poorly designed, unfriendly interfaces. Thankfully, most (but not all) major sites nowadays offer their clients a fast, reliable and intuitive gaming experience. Incidentally, you may notice that sometimes when one site is experiencing Internet problems, several other sites also suffer downtime. There is nothing untoward about this – many poker sites have servers located in the same facility, so connection problems affecting one site are likely to be affecting other sites as well.

Although UltimateBet is the only site to offer its clients the choice of two entirely different interfaces (Standard View and the innovative and attractive MiniView™), most sites do offer drop-down menus to enable you to adapt some elements of the interface to your desire. For example, you may find that for some sites the speed of your connection is improved if you remove the 'animation' features using the tabs in the lobby. In addition, some players (myself included) prefer to utilise the 'four-colour deck' option where this choice is available. This may enable you to identify the suits quicker and more accurately, especially if you are playing multiple tables and need to be able to distinguish the suits of the cards at a very brief glance.

Nearly all online sites have been designed primarily for the Windows environment. However, Apple Macintosh and Linux users can either choose to play at a site such as Pokerroom.com, where no download is required, or invest in an emulator program such as VirtualPC for Macintosh, which will enable them to access any online site.

Automatic All-ins

From time to time, either you or one of your opponents will experience server or PC problems during a hand, and will be unable to act in turn due to a lag, disconnection or freeze. Depending on the site in question, that player may be put automatically all-in at that point for the chips they have already committed to the pot, able to win the main pot, but excluded from any side pot that may be created. The idea is to protect players from losing their investment in a pot just because of connectivity problems – sometimes such disconnections will work in favour of the player and sometimes against. Of course, if you suspect that someone is abusing the all-in protection rule, deliberately disconnecting themselves in a difficult situation to avoid having to call a bet, you should report them to the support team.

Many sites do not allow automatic all-ins for pot-limit and no-limit games – it is important to check the specific rules for that site if you intend to participate in such games. In fact, in the past couple of years many of the major sites have removed the automatic all-in facility even for limit games. Even on those sites where automatic all-ins are still allowed, players are only allowed a given quota of all-ins (typically one or two) within a 24-hour period; once that quota has expired any further disconnections are likely to result in a loss of the pot by default. However, most sites do have an all-in reset procedure whereby players can request that their all-ins be restored. If your all-in quota expires, it is important to request a reset straightaway, since otherwise you may end up needlessly forfeiting a big pot if your prevailing connection problems persist.

Shuffling

'Trust everyone, and always cut the cards.' W.C. Fields, actor

Over the past few years one of the most controversial areas of debate in Internet poker has been the issue of online shuffling. Clearly the purpose of any fair shuffle is to create a random deck such that every possible sequence of cards is possible, while at the same time making it impossible for anyone to predict the position of any card in the deck. In principle, unless they are crooked or contain bugs, online shuffles should be closer to random than can possibly be achieved in a live-action game, where the cards are often just collected, riffled a couple of times and dealt, with the result that clumps of cards can sometimes stay together. As an example, the Paradise Poker website states that: 'No deck of cards in any brick and mortar cardroom is ever shuffled as well and as thoroughly as we shuffle our cards. Each game, the deck is shuffled 10 times with each shuffle moving each card between one and 51 times throughout the deck ... There is no bias to any card, any card patterns or seats at the table.'

However, the key rider here is *unless they are crooked or contain bugs*. In the early days of online poker, the shuffling algorithm for the ASF Software Inc. Hold'em games, used in at least three online cardrooms (including Planet Poker), was far from flawless. In September 1999 the Software Security Group at Reliable Software Technologies uncovered a means of calculating the precise deck being used for each hand, knowledge of which would have enabled unscrupulous cheats to know in advance the exact hands of every player, together with the future cards that would be dealt in that hand. Unfortunately, the 'seed' (or particular starting point) used for the ASF Software random number generator at that time was the number of milliseconds since midnight according to the system clock, which thus made it easily predictable once the RST program was synchronised with the system clock; and RST also identified other flaws in the shuffling algorithm. Of course, these problems were quickly addressed by the online card-rooms affected, but the fact that a shuffling algorithm had been cracked was very damaging for the credibility of the online poker industry as a whole at that time.

Nowadays every online cardroom is acutely aware of the need to reassure their clients that their shuffle is fair, random and unpredictable. A visit to the website of any of these companies will reveal the different ways in which they generate their shuffles. Clearly, the understanding and implementation of these complicated processes has moved on considerably since 1999, in particular with regard to the criteria used in selecting the seed used in random number generation, and shuffling has become more secure. However, that does not necessarily mean that it is absolutely foolproof at every single site.

Many newcomers to online poker, on experiencing an initial run of bad results, rush to blame their losses on unfair shuffling (or on collusion by other players – see the section on 'Cheating') rather than questioning their own play. Undoubtedly it is possible to write software that gives the cardroom an edge in some way, perhaps by juicing the deck to produce more 'action' hands and thereby maximising the rake. The key question is whether it would be worth any major online site becoming involved in such a practice – their existing rake income is generally quite sufficient to keep their businesses running smoothly, so why would they risk such a practice in case they were found out (perhaps through being outed by a disaffected ex-employee) and lost their entire business?

Although it is true that online cardrooms survive by extracting money from their clients, it is in their long-term interests to do so honestly via the rake rather than dishonestly by cheating. Whether you are a long-term winner or a long-term loser, you will contribute more or less the same hourly rake over time, and companies with a satisfied strong regular player base (many of whom will then recommend the site to their friends) can expect large revenue returns for many years to come. Of course, it is not impossible that decks are being 'juiced', but there is no hard evidence to suggest that such practices are in operation.

One common complaint on poker forums and newsgroups is that players are drawn out on more online, with the online shuffle somehow generating more river cards that defeat made hands. Regardless of whether this complaint is actually justified (it may just seem like you are being drawn out on more because so many more hands are dealt per hour online than in a live-action cardroom, and so many hands are dealt with a full ten players seated at the table), being drawn out on is the natural occupational hazard of the winning player. One of the key advantages of most winning players over their fellow competitors is that they consistently enter the pot with better average starting holdings, so they will need to be drawn out on more often if they are to lose. In the meantime, they are being paid off handsomely on numerous other occasions by weaker players who are staying in the pot with poor odds, hoping to hit longshot draws.

Another common newsgroup and forum online poker myth is the so-called 'cash-out curse'. Many players seem to believe that when they cash-out from a site this will somehow lead to them being flagged by the cardroom and dealt a higher than average number of losing hands. This myth can be debunked in many ways, including the following:

♠ At any point in time you are on either a good run or a bad run, with wins following losses and losses following wins. Inevitably, when you are on a good run you are more likely to cash-out and will subsequently appear to experience the 'cash-out' curse when the law of averages comes into play and your inevitable bad run arrives. When these players perceive that they are being afflicted with the cash-out curse, they are merely experiencing a natural regression towards the mean. Furthermore, those who are fortunate enough to maintain their good run after a cash-out will never have cause to report it; it is only those who lose after a cash-out who ever publish their experiences, and in so doing, perpetuate the myth.

♠ When you experience a good run and cash-out, you may start to play in over-confident fashion, overplaying your hands and generally failing to pay as much attention to the game as you did before. Inevitably, this then manifests itself in a losing run.

♠ Often when players cash-out they leave themselves with an inadequate bankroll, which is then vulnerable to the natural short-term swings of the limit at which they are playing.

♠ There is no real financial reason why a site should dislike players who cash-out, but nevertheless continue to play at the site regularly. Whether individual players are winners or losers is basically irrelevant to the cardroom, so long as they keep coming back and thereby maintain their contribution to the rake.

To date no evidence has ever been produced to suggest that the shuffle at any online poker site is any way rigged. At Paradise Poker the shuffle is reviewed on a quarterly basis by Price Waterhouse Coopers. Using the log files provided, PWC have performed a series of statistical tests and affirmed that in their opinion every card has an equal chance of being selected. Furthermore, many newsgroup posters have also independently analysed the hand histories from Paradise Poker and other sites, using samples of 60,000 hands or more, and drawn the same conclusions.

Cheating

'The biggest enemy of poker is cheating.' Mason Malmuth, *Poker Essays, Volume III*

Without question many people are reluctant to play on the Internet for fear of being cheated, either by the cardroom or (more likely) by other players. Barely a week goes by without some anonymous poster on one poker forum or another telling how he was 'cheated' online in some way or another. Invariably the thrust of their argument is something along the lines of 'I've been playing for 20 years and I've never seen so many bad beats. I know I'm a good poker player, so if I'm losing then the game can't possibly be on the level.' Although on occasion these complaints do turn out to be perfectly valid, in the vast majority of cases the players involved are almost certainly victims of misfortune (or their own bad play) rather than cheating. Furthermore, since there are plenty of other players who claim that they do win at online poker sites without having to resort to cheating – are we to assume that they do so only because they are such brilliant players that they can overcome stacked decks and collusion teams? It is true that most players lose when they play poker at an online cardroom, but then again most players lose when they play poker in a brick and mortar cardroom as well (the mathematics of the rake practically guarantees that this be so).

In July 2002 pokerpages.com published an excellent article by Andrew Glazer on this very subject, entitled 'Ten Reasons Why You're Not Getting Cheated Online'. His argument was not that cheating does not go on (indeed he stated that he was sure that in certain instances players had colluded with one another), but that there are alternative explanations for poker losses that players often ignore, preferring instead to blame someone else rather than themselves. Glazer offered the following possible explanations as to why players might experience (or appear to experience) worse results online than they do in a brick and mortar cardroom:

♠ Players are forced to keep better records online. When you receive your monthly credit card bill it is pretty hard to fool yourself that you have had a winning month when you have actually lost, whereas live-action players who don't keep accurate records may imagine that they are winning players even when they are not. As Glazer says, 'Many players who think they are break-even players in live games are actually losers, and many players who think they are winning players are actually break-even or losing players.' Thus some players may only be imagining that their results are worse online; better record-keeping would reveal that their live-action results are comparable.

♠ Online play removes much of the skill involved in reading people from the game. Those players for whom tells and other people-reading skills are a vital element of their game will not be able to achieve such good results online. For such players Glazer eloquently suggests that 'when you play online you have two arms and one leg tied behind your back.'

♠ Many players don't concentrate as hard when they play online as they would in a brick and mortar cardroom. By engaging in multi-tasking while you are playing online, perhaps watching TV, answering e-mails or surfing the Internet, you will not collect as much information about the other players as you would in a live game, and this will inevitably have a negative effect on your results.

♠ Many more hands are played per hour online than in a live-action game (perhaps giving the misleading impression that more bad beats are occurring). If you are already a losing player, then faster games will inevitably cause you to lose more every hour you play online (although this may partially be off-set by the lower rake and the absence of tipping).

♠ The nature of the online game sometimes encourages players to play more loosely than they normally would. The simple physical act of clicking on a mouse rather than counting out chips and placing them in the pot may cause players to enter and stay in more hands, often calling to the river with hands they would fold in a live-action game. Furthermore, there is no peer pressure to play 'properly': if you play an online hand badly and still somehow manage to win, you don't have to endure any muttering or dirty looks from the other players, all tacitly censuring you for playing so poorly.

♠ If the game is indeed looser than a normal brick and mortar game, then more players will stay to the river and more 'miracle' bad beats will arise as a result.

♠ If the game is already looser than a normal game, then it may become even looser as additional players are sucked into every hand by the prospect of winning a large pot if they hit a big hand.

♠ Players are more prone to going on tilt online. We have already discussed the phenomenon of cybertilt, whereby players are more likely to lose their composure and steam off their bankrolls when there is no-one watching them.

♠ Players can run into more problems when they play two tables simultaneously. Again, we have already discussed this concept. It is harder for multi-table players to keep track of their opponents' tendencies, while playing two or more tables at once can be particularly dangerous for players who have a tendency to go on tilt.

♠ Players may play differently because they are paranoid that they are being cheated, making detrimental adjustments to their decisions merely because they fear the worst.

Having listed some of the reasons why players may not be being cheated when they believe that they are, it is now time to consider ways in which cheating can (and occasionally does) go on.

Collusion

'I believe collusion at poker is not just unsportsmanlike and wrong, it's a very serious crime.' Mike Caro

Undoubtedly, the form of cheating that most players fear is collusion. This might be two players at the same table revealing their hole cards to one another via the telephone or Instant Messenger, or just a single player playing two hands in the same game from the same location (using two accounts, two phone lines and two PCs), perhaps raising with one hand and re-raising with another to force other players out of the pot. Indeed, it is theoretically possible to imagine a scenario in which every other player at the table apart from you could actually be sitting in the same Internet cafe!

However, it is important to note that even if you know the hole cards of another player, or have the facility to raise and reraise with two hands in the same game, it still requires a fairly high degree of poker skill to be able to utilise this to defeat the other players at the table. It is quite likely that many poor players might still lose even if they were to cheat, and misjudged attempts at collusion could actually cause some of them to lose more than they would playing 'straight'! Furthermore, it is much less likely that you will come across any cheating at the lower limits. One has to wonder whether an adept collusion team would bother with games lower than, say, $5/$10 – if you have made up your mind to cheat, one assumes that you would do so for large enough stakes to make it worthwhile, given the risk of getting caught and potentially having your account closed and bankroll frozen. One would also imagine that short-handed games are more vulnerable to online cardsharps than full ring games, since it is easier to cheat two or three players than eight, and in short-handed play every player is involved in far more pots, so any collusion partnership would be presented with that many more opportunities to cheat.

It is also worth bearing in mind the fact that collusion is not just an online phenomenon – it has been a problem since poker was invented. Just as it is a concern for online cardrooms nowadays, it has also been a problem at some live-action games in the past, with unsuspecting players running into teams of colluders exchanging information about their hands via verbal codes or hand signals.

There are only two ways to combat the cheats: extreme vigilance by the players and security measures from the cardroom. If you suspect that two or more players may be colluding, you have a responsibility both to yourself and to other players to report these suspicions to the cardroom for investigation. At a brick and mortar cardroom, security staff have the advantage of being able to watch the players, and in particular observe how they interact with one another. Although online cardrooms do not have this facility, they do have the important option of being able to go back and scrutinise everyone's hole cards for any hand that might be deemed worthy of investigation. Furthermore, most online cardrooms claim to possess sophisticated software that can automatically pinpoint other suspicious activities, such as abnormally high win rates. For example, at Paradise Poker the following measures are in place, quoting from an e-mail I received from their support team in the summer of 2002:

Our Security Department makes use of the following preventative measures:

1. Tracking IP address and matching historical playing patterns. This flags and determines if certain players historically play on the same table.

2. Player trapping monitoring. Historical hands are automatically reviewed and if a weak hand was involved with raising and re-raising with multiple players it is flagged and forwarded to security.

3. Strong hand folding. If a player folds a strong hand before the flop such as AQ when another player has AK it is flagged.

4. Any player that reports a suspicious hand, it is thoroughly reviewed by our security dept. Security will also review the historical hands of the players involved. It is this ability to see every player's entire history that gives us the incredible ability to combat collusion better than a brick and mortar cardroom.

There are also additional automated features that I have declined to mention, given that making such measures public would essentially defeat their purpose … We are under no illusion that in order for us to be successful we need to grow our client base and have positive word of mouth, this could never be accomplished if the games were not conducted in a totally fair and honest environment.

There have been instances in the past where proven colluders have had their accounts frozen, and players whom the cardroom believes may possibly have been colluding (without possessing any concrete proof) are often barred from sitting at the same table together in future. However, there have also undoubtedly been many instances in which colluders have managed to evade detection. It is unlikely that cheating can ever be completely eradicated from poker (either in its online or live-action forms), but if players remain vigilant and report any suspicious activities, thereby helping to police the game themselves, then hopefully any colluders can be identified and barred from the game.

All-In Abuse

We have already discussed the problems that can arise when a player does not act in the allotted time during a hand. At some sites, the player is put all-in for the money that has already been placed in the pot, and the other players carry on contesting a side pot for the rest of the hand. It is almost always the case that these automatic all-in situations arise because the player has been unintentionally disconnected from the game, due either to Internet routing problems or a computer crash. However, from time to time the automatic all-in privilege is abused by unscrupulous players choosing to deliberately disconnect themselves rather than having to make a difficult call in a big pot. (Of course, this is an even greater problem in pot-limit and no-limit games, where the last bet could amount to a considerable amount of money.) At PokerStars and Paradise Poker, for example, if you time out and are still connected to the game server, then your hand is automatically folded, but it still is a matter for the individual cardroom to decide whether that disconnect was intentional or accidental. Clearly if you suspect that anyone has abused the all-in rule, the onus is on you to report the incident to the cardroom for investigation (ideally with a note of the hand number so that they can track it down easily). All-in abuse is cheating, and there have been several instances in which players have been barred from a cardroom for this practice.

Programmer Cheats

Although collusion and all-in abuses are the most prevalent problems, there are other security issues which discourage some people from playing online. One common fear is that someone may be able to see your hole cards. This may be either because the original programmer has revealed the 'key' to the encryption algorithm to a cheat, enabling him to see everyone's hole cards, or because someone has somehow managed to break into the server and bypass the code. (Players are recommended to provide themselves with an extra measure of protection by installing firewalls on their PCs.) Alternatively, the programmer may have disclosed the shuffling algorithm, enabling a cheat to determine which cards are likely to come next. Finally, the programmer may have left a backdoor into the software to enable him to insert hidden code to enable certain designated players to win. Although these means of cheating are possible, there has never been an instance in which anything like this has ever actually happened – it would be so damaging for any cardroom to fall victim to this kind of cheating that it is hard to believe that adequate security measures would not be in place.

Clamping down on the Cheats

Although they are in business competition with one another, if the major sites were able to get together and share their information about known cheaters, and even discuss methods of tracking down cheaters in future, they would undoubtedly be doing a great service both to themselves, and to the online poker-playing community as a whole. A firmer, across-the-board approach to the problem of cheating would encourage new players to participate and give existing players the confidence to compete for higher stakes. Indeed, according to Paradise Poker's head of marketing Bruce Davidson (quoted in an article in the *New York Times* from November 2001) one reason why the site has been reluctant to raise the maximum stakes, is precisely because they are concerned that this would attract more sophisticated cheaters and hackers.

Furthermore, it is not sufficient that cheaters be barred; each site should adopt an open policy of refunding losses to players who have been the victims of proven cheating. Although both PokerStars and

Planet Poker, for example, have refunded cheated players in the past, this does not appear to be a universal policy among cardrooms at the present time. Short-sightedly, some sites may prefer not to admit that any specific acts of collusion have arisen, whereas a more open treatment of such instances would demonstrate not only that they hold a powerful stance against collusion, but also that they possess the resources to detect and combat it. In this way, they would not only reinforce public confidence in their commitment towards honest games, but also discourage potential cheats.

Online Poker Robots

Apart from collusion, another common fear that many players have when they play online, is that they might be playing against poker robots (autonomous poker-playing computer programs) rather than humans. The concern is that with modern programming techniques, these robots (controlled either by the cardroom or independently by other players) could possibly play poker at such a high level that they can beat the game consistently. Whereas losing money at poker to another human is unpleasant, most players would regard losing money to a computer as being cheated. There are essentially three issues to address with regard to these robots ('bots'):

♠ Is it feasible that computers could play better poker than most humans?

♠ Does such software already exist?

♠ Are bots necessarily a bad thing?

The Feasibility of Online Poker Bots

Until recently, the most powerful commercially available poker programs were those produced by Wilson Software. Although these programs are quite sophisticated, with extremely good instructional modules, the best human players can defeat these programs consistently. Why? Because poker is not just a game of probability and statistics, it is also a game of reading people. Whereas sophisticated computer programs are excellent at the former, it is in the latter area that they fall down, which is why poker programs have not yet been able to match the success of 'Jellyfish' in backgammon and 'Deep Blue' in chess. How do you program a computer to sense when other players are on tilt, playing too passively or aggressively, or bluffing too much? That is the key challenge that the programmers face if bots are ever to be able to defeat the world's best poker players.

Does such Software already exist?

Although it is not entirely inconceivable that online bots are already being used to win consistently against very good players, this would appear to be unlikely at the present time. In the past couple of years there have been several attempts to market bots which play online. Most notably the developers of the Winholdem program have been involved in a long-running cat-and-mouse battle with the major online cardrooms, trying to enable its bot to operate undetected. According to PartyPoker's general manager Vikrant Bhargava in a recent interview: 'There are a few commercially available programs which people have tried to use. We make a change and these guys again try to beat the system. With our last update, I believe we have rendered the commercially available bots useless.' Be warned – the major sites may well confiscate your online funds if you are detected running an online bot.

The University of Alberta poker research team has been working on its 'Poki' program for many years. Although it is quite a sophisticated program, the researchers have claimed that 'Poki plays a reasonably good game of poker, but there remains considerable research to be done to play at a world-class level.' In fact, 'Poki' has now been developed into a commercially available software program, Poker Academy Pro, which functions well both as entertainment and as a learning tool.

Having said that, the potential financial rewards from developing an online bot that is capable of winning consistently at $5/$10 or above are immense, so it is far from impossible that it could happen one day, perhaps in heads-up play, where there is only one opponent to read and poker is reduced to its most basic components.

Are Bots necessarily a Bad Thing?

Many people automatically assume that poker bots are a negative development in the game. However, this is not necessarily the case. At

UltimateBet bots were used to fill up the play money tables for many years, so that anyone could practise their play, day or night, sure in the knowledge that there would be opponents to play against. Indeed, Mike Caro has gone on record as saying that, although there are no bots at the site he used to endorse (Planet Poker) he is not necessarily averse to using them to start games, so long as they are clearly identified and guaranteed not to win (or if they were to win, then the money would be returned to the players through promotions). However, if bots were one day able to defeat the best human players regularly, this would naturally be very detrimental to online cardrooms, since no-one would bother playing unless they had access to an equally powerful bot themselves. The online game would eventually be reduced to just computer against computer.

Indeed, in July 2005 the concept of 'poker machine vs. poker machine' was put to the test at the first World Poker Robot Championship in Las Vegas, which carried a $100,000 first prize. The winning program was 'PokerProbot', designed by Hilton Givens, a car salesman and software developer from Lafayette. PokerProbot defeated five other computers and went on to challenge WPT winner Phil Laak in a heads-up match. Thankfully for mankind, the human emerged victorious after three hour's play.

The Scoop Monster Experiment

Billed as 'Hand analysis for serious poker players', the launch of the Scoop Monster program at the beginning of October 2002 caused something of a furore in the online poker world. The program, which worked exclusively with the True Poker playing client, was designed to tell players the precise odds of winning the current hand, and advise them how to proceed. Not only that, but Scoop Monster could also be set to automatically play the hand for you! Naturally the arrival of a 'bot-like' program such as this provoked a great deal of interest and debate, not least at True Poker itself, who were as surprised as anyone by its appearance, since they had no affiliation with Scoop Monster whatsoever.

Players who experimented with Scoop Monster on True Poker generally reported one slight flaw in the 'autoplay' features – it just didn't play very well! Although it was able to hold its own in play money games, it is doubtful whether anyone could hope to make a worth-

worthwhile long-term profit with the original version of the program in real money games. Despite this fact, True Poker understandably saw the new program as a threat to their business, which hinges on the concept of real players competing against one another for real money, and rapidly implemented countermeasures against the product. Not only did they announce software changes to prevent players from using Scoop Monster, but they also announced a clear policy that anyone found to be using this or similar programs would have their accounts terminated. By the end of October, Scoop Monster had been taken off the market; all that remained was a message on the Scoop Monster website stating that the product was no longer available and that all existing customers were being reimbursed.

Online Tournaments

Multi-Table or sit and go?

In the past twenty years, tournament poker has become hugely popular around the world, not least because it is an ideal way for newcomers to familiarise themselves with the game. First of all, your maximum financial risk is known in advance. For example, if you enter a $10 no-limit hold'em tournament at PokerStars your liability is limited to $11 ($10 buy-in for the prize pool plus a $1 registration fee for the house). Second, the potential reward is always much greater than the entry fee, so everyone has an incentive to try their best. Third, online tournaments typically deal at over twice the rate of their brick and mortar counterparts, so there is a lot more play to them. Finally, tournaments are tremendous fun – over the course of an event your stack of chips can go through wild fluctuations; you can inflict and receive bizarre bad beats on all-in bets etc. Many players love the cut and thrust and adrenaline rush of tournaments, and find cash games something of a grind in comparison.

Online tournaments come in two distinct forms: single-table (often called 'sit and go') events, in which typically nine or ten players (eight for seven-card stud) compete against each other, and multiple-table events, which may contain dozens or hundreds of entrants. Nowadays most sites offer both single- and multi-table events, but some specialise in one or the other. And likewise some players prefer single-table events, others multi-table and many play both types.

Sit and Go Tournaments

For a sit and go event there is no pre-determined start time – you simply pay your entry fee, take your seat and wait for the table to fill up with other players before you can start (which may sometimes take quite a while, depending on the time of day and overall site traffic!). Typically, a single-table sit and go tourney will last a maximum of an hour or so and pay out on the first three places (50% for the winner, 30% for second and 20% for third), but you should ensure that you check the prize structure before you start play. In addition to the standard single-table events, PokerStars also offers two-table sit and go events with 18 players (16 for stud) and four prizes.

At some sites the sit and go blind structure is such that the blinds rise very rapidly (every ten hands), and players are forced to take risks almost from the outset. Some purists find these games unattractive, reasoning that this turns the tournament into something of a crap-shoot. However, there is no doubt that at sites with a relatively more sedate blind structure (such as PokerStars, where there are only nine players, the blinds go up every ten minutes rather than every ten hands, and everyone starts with a fairly large stack of chips) sit and go events can be a lucrative, fast-moving and enjoyable avenue for many players. Indeed, Mike Caro argues that for good players short tournaments may prove more profitable than larger tournaments in the long run, because:

♠ They provide an excellent opportunity to exploit skill differentials.

♠ You can play two or more shorter tournaments in the time it would take to reach the final of a single long event, thus reducing the 'luck' component.

♠ You risk proportionately less of your bankroll on each individual event.

To these factors, I would add a fourth:

♠ Single-table tournaments are great practice for the final tables of multi-table events!

Multiple-Table Tournaments

Unlike sit and go tournaments, which start whenever there is a full table, multiple-table events are always scheduled in advance. Usually registration will begin an hour or more before the start of the event and will close either when the first person is eliminated, when all the tables are full or at a designated time after the start. As more and more players are eliminated, the tables are merged until ultimately there is only one table left, at which point the event takes on the characteristics of a single-table event. Typically a multi-table event will last for several hours and offer a much longer prize list than its single-table counterpart; it is very common for every player who reaches the final table to receive a prize if there are around 45 or more entries.

Nowadays most of the major cardrooms offer re-buy tournaments, in addition to the traditional freezeout events. Re-buy tournaments are attractive because in general, the cardroom does not take a cut when you re-buy or add-on (Paradise Poker being a notable exception to this). Furthermore, with more chips in play than a normal event, there is more play to it (although this does mean that it will go on longer!).

Inspired by the example of Chris Moneymaker, who turned a $39 PokerStars satellite into $2.5 million at the World Series of Poker, most sites now offer satellites for the major brick and mortar events. Not just for the WSOP, but also for the World Poker Tour and many other events. These satellites are hugely popular. After all, who can resist the thought that for as little as $1, they could be rubbing shoulders with Doyle Brunson and Gus Hansen, playing for a huge prize at the final table of a nationally televised event!

One advantage of multiple-table online tournaments over their brick and mortar equivalents is that you are usually provided with completely up-to-date information on where you stand in the tournament, how many players are left, and the relative chip positions of all the remaining players. This valuable information can and should be used to help you formulate your strategy for reaching the final table and beyond! At PokerStars can go to the tournament lobby for the full picture on where you stand at that particular point in time (although information on your current position and the largest and smallest stack can be obtained by clicking the 'Info' tab).

Nowadays some sites allow players to do prize-money deals for the top places. These are usually negotiated through the chat boxes and then relayed to the site's support team. Needless to say, you should check beforehand that the site at which you are playing permits deals, involve the tournament director if at all possible, immediately notify support of the deal that has been struck so that they can transfer the funds, and ensure that you are able to provide back-up evidence (in case someone should renege on the deal) by keeping a copy of the chat. During the first World Championship of Online Poker in July 2002, PokerStars actually provided the facility to pause the tournament (if all the remaining players agreed) so that deals could be discussed.

There have been numerous incidents in multi-table tournaments in which one player has deliberately employed 'stalling' tactics (using the maximum allotted time allowed for each decision) with, say, two tables left in order to improve their chances of a higher placing. There are three possible ways in which stalling might benefit a player: first, the players on another table might simply knock each other out, enabling the stalling player to reach the final table; second, a rise in the blinds may occur that will cause someone else to be forced to go all-in before the player who is doing the stalling; and finally, a middle stack might stall to prevent a big stack from running over the table whilst everyone is in a defensive mode, hoping to make the final table. It is conventional for tournaments to go to 'hand for hand' just prior to the formation of the final table. This combats the first and third stalling methods but not the second. Although legal, such angle-shooting tactics are not to be recommended and may very well incur the wrath of fellow players if taken to extremes.

Another possible angle that sometimes arises in tournaments is 'chip-dumping', whereby one player deliberately loses all their chips to another in order to enhance the latter's tournament prospects. Tournament action is so fast and furious that chip-dumping is far from easy to detect while you are playing. However, if you suspect that another player is being assisted in this way, then you should protect yourself and the other players in the tournament by notifying support of your suspicions.

Freeroll Tournaments

Many sites offer regular freeroll events to attract new players and encourage existing players to return to the site on a regular basis. These may be either 'true' freerolls with no entry conditions whatsoever, or perks for players who have already provided the cardroom with a certain amount of patronage (typically measured by the number of raked hands in which they have participated).

The challenge for the cardroom is to structure these freeroll tournaments in such a way that they are attractive enough for players to visit the site, but not so attractive that their clientele will spend all their poker sessions playing freerolls at the expense of raked ring games or buy-in tournaments! Undoubtedly, some players who play in freeroll tournaments do so with no intention of ever depositing any cash to play in real money games, but even these players have some value to the cardroom, since they may encourage their friends to join the site, and those players may then make deposits and in turn encourage their own friends to sign up. A true freeroll tournament at, for example, PokerStars will attract 250-500 players, offering newcomers an ideal introduction to online tournament play.

There are two contrasting ways of approaching a freeroll event – you can either try and play your best game, treating it as a serious exercise, or you can decide to take lots of risks early on, figuring that you could get lucky and amass a ton of chips, but if you bust out you haven't lost anything anyway!

Profitability

'The winner of any poker tournament always got lucky – online or in a real-world casino.' Mike Caro

Just as there are many online players who make a very good return on their efforts in cash games, so there are others who prefer to focus on tournaments. Many events contain a proportion of players who lack the bankroll and/or skills to be successful in cash play and prefer to take a shot at a decent prize for a small investment. Occasionally a multiple-table tournament will be won by a relatively weak player scoring a one-off triumph, but in general the better players naturally can expect a clear positive expectation. Over the course of a whole event, the combined skills of the better players should overwhelm those of a weaker player. The latter may have a good run and win some sizable pots, but even if they eliminate some of the good players there will usually still be enough decent players left with sufficient chips to ensure that they will most likely come unstuck in the end. Furthermore, part of the success of the top players in large buy-in ($100 or more) events is that they have developed very good reads on the other regular players in these events, which enables them to make the kind of profitable opponent-specific plays that would be impossible for a less experienced rival.

It is often argued that good tournament players should be able to make at least a 40-50% return on their investment in the long run (i.e. $4-$5 profit for every $10 spent on buy-ins), and there are undoubtedly some online tournament specialists who are able to make 100%, particularly for low buy-in events. However, it is important to remember that the variance attached to tournament play is high – in the short run one big tournament victory could make all the difference in determining whether a player is ahead of the game or not. Furthermore, the short-term luck factor involved in tournament play can be quite high, especially for sit and go tournaments in which the blinds escalate rapidly, thereby possibly nullifying some of the edge of the better players.

The long run in tournament play might therefore be defined as at least 100 events – until you have played this many tournaments, your results will not be a particularly reliable indicator of whether or not you can beat the game in the long run. Indeed, if you specialise in multi-table events, and your results are such that you nearly always finish outside the money, punctuated by the occasional big pay-off, even 100 tournaments is too few to be regarded as a reliable sample size. For this reason, an absolute bare minimum bankroll of 20 buy-ins is probably necessary for a serious tournament player, and it is perhaps advisable to keep as many as 50 buy-ins in your bankroll if you play exclusively in multi-table events.

Nowadays many players like to specialise in the widely available sit and go events. With the normal 50%/30%/20% prize structure in these tournaments, each player starts with a theoretical 30% chance of making the prize list (assuming the standard ten-player tables). However, since the cardroom usually charges 10% of each buy-in in registration fees, you would actually need to reach the final three 33% of the time to break even (assuming you achieve an equal ratio of first places to seconds to thirds). Undoubtedly, specialists at the lower buy-in levels (e.g. $10 and $20) have the long-term potential to cash out considerably more than 33% of the time, possibly as much as 50% for a very good player and 60% for a really top-flight player at this level. Furthermore, it is highly likely that their tournament skills would enable them to achieve a higher number of first place finishes relative to seconds and thirds, thereby increasing their overall level of profitability.

In a newsgroup post a few years back, WSOP bracelet-winner Daniel Negreanu claimed that he had played 85 $100 single-table tournaments at Paradise Poker the year before, winning 16, and placing second 11 times and third seven times for a 40% cash-out ratio and an average profit of just over $40 per event. However, the blinds in the Paradise Poker tournaments rise so quickly (every ten hands) that tournaments typically last only 70-90 hands, which almost certainly would have negated some of his ability and allowed the weaker players more of a chance. It is quite conceivable that in multi-table events (or sit and go events with a different blind structure) his return would be considerably greater than this.

Whichever type of tournament you choose to play, you should always ensure that:

♠ Your connection is in good order before you start. There is nothing more frustrating than being disconnected during a tournament and anted-away while you are trying to return to the game.

♠ You will not be disturbed while you are playing. Any distractions will cause you to lose focus, and if you are called away from the table you will again be anted-away.

♠ You have organised some refreshments in advance, particularly for a multi-table event, which could easily last several hours.

♠ Everyone else is present at the table when you start play. If any players are absent then you can steal their blinds without mercy. Also, watch out for anyone who joins your table midway through a tournament – if they happen to be sitting out and the other players don't notice immediately, then you can steal their blinds too!

Chapter Four

Selecting an Online Cardroom

'I put three kids through college playing poker. Unfortunately, they weren't my kids.' Max Shapiro

Introduction

Once you have taken the decision to play poker online, the next important question you will face is: Where should I play? There are many factors that need to be considered when selecting an online cardroom, of which the following are probably the most significant (in no particular order):

Does it offer the form of poker that I prefer to play?

Some poker sites offer a fairly limited selection of games, whereas others have a wide array. If you are a hold'em player, then every site should be able to cater for you, but other games are not so widely spread. Tables 1 and 2 later in this chapter list the games on offer at each major site. Note that at some sites the less popular games rarely actually run, even though they may be on offer.

Does it offer the right limits for me?

If you are a low-limit hold'em full ring-game player, then you will have no problem finding a game somewhere or other. However, if you wish to play high stakes, short-handed or heads-up, or other games apart from hold'em, then you may have to look further afield for suitable sites at which to play. Table 3 offers a site-by-site comparison of the limit games available at each site, and Table 4 focuses on pot-limit and no-limit games.

Are the rakes and tournament registration fees reasonable?

In general, the rakes for online ring games are highly competitive compared to brick and mortar cardrooms. However, they do vary from site to site, and it is worth considering the rake when selecting a place to play (see Tables 5 and 6).

Does it offer the kind of tournaments I like?

Nowadays every major site offers both single-table and multi-table tournaments. However, the number of starting chips and the blind structure can vary greatly from site to site, which will affect the amount of 'play' there is in a tournament.

Are there sufficient games running at the times at which I want to play?

Most major sites offer a selection of games at peak hours, but can be fairly quiet outside those times. The busiest period of the day to play for every major site is between the hours of 8pm and 10pm EST (5pm-7pm PST; 1am-3am GMT). The main exception to this is Ladbrokes, which is busiest between 3pm and 6pm EST (12pm-3pm PST; 8pm-11pm GMT). If you are based in Europe you may therefore wish to consider Ladbrokes, where the absence of US-based players means that their peak traffic occurs in the early evening European time. It may also be worth considering the biggest site, PartyPoker, which is constantly busy 24 hours a day. Dennis Boyko's poker traffic measurement site at pokerpulse.com carries up-to-date information on how many players are playing at each major site.

Is it well-established and financially secure, and publicly supported by people whose reputations you respect?

Since the vast majority of online cardrooms are based offshore, it is impossible to know whether your funds are really secure. However, it is common sense to restrict your deposits to sites that are already well-established and are experiencing a solid (and increasing) flow of traffic. In order to enhance their credibility, many sites have chosen to associate with leading figures in the poker world, for example Full Tilt Poker with Howard Lederer, Phil Ivey and a host of other top poker players, PokerStars with Tom McEvoy, UltimateBet with Phil Hellmuth, Annie Duke, Russ Hamilton et al, and PartyPoker with Mike Sexton. Clearly these personalities have long-standing reputations that they would not want to see tarnished, so their endorsement must count for something, even if it is by no means a guarantee that the site is 100% safe.

Where is the site located?

Since US laws currently prevent any Internet gambling companies from operating within its borders, cardrooms are forced to operate offshore. Many have therefore opted to base themselves in Costa Rica, taking advantage of its relatively lax banking laws and geographical proximity to the US. Internet gambling companies are legal in Costa Rica, provided that betting money from abroad is not deposited in Costa Rican bank accounts. Indeed, local officials have estimated that there are as many as two hundred gambling firms currently based in downtown San Jose!

Is it backed up by good customer support?

From time to time you will find that you have an issue that needs to be resolved by the cardroom's support team. It could be that you are having difficulties transferring money into or out of your account, are experiencing problems with the software, wish to report your suspicions that two players are colluding, or simply would like to put forward a suggestion as to how the site might be improved. Whatever the matter at hand, you need to feel confident that the cardroom will deal competently and promptly with your enquiry.

By definition online poker takes place in a 'virtual' world, so there is no human face to turn to if a problem does arise. It is therefore even more vital that, in order to retain the goodwill of their clients, online cardrooms deal promptly and efficiently with any complaints or queries that may arise. From time to time the customer support team of one site or another will be subjected to an attack by a disaffected client on a poker newsgroup or forum. Sometimes the complaint will indeed be justified, but on other occasions the poster is merely seeking revenge against the cardroom, having broken their rules and been caught (and perhaps even had his account frozen), and left with no other means of venting his anger than to sound off against the cardroom in public. Naturally, it is in the interests of the cardrooms to avoid any bad publicity if at all possible, and many use newsgroups and forums to respond openly to legitimate queries, complaints and suggestions.

Some sites offer a live floorperson facility, whereby players can call a customer support representative to the table, whereas other sites rely on e-mail support and/or toll-free telephone numbers. None of these methods is inherently superior to another – the only important factor is whether the client's query is adequately dealt with. Many players actually prefer to use the e-mail method, since many enquiries are impossible to resolve straightaway, and live floorperson and phone conversations often end with the statement that 'we'll have to get back to you on that', thereby leaving the client feeling somewhat in limbo.

Is it easy to deposit funds and cash-out?

One disadvantage of online cardrooms compared to regular ones, is that you can't take your chips to the cashier at the end of a session and walk away with the cash. In the current environment, particularly in the US, most credit card companies prevent their clients from making Internet gambling-related deposits and withdrawals. It is therefore vital that real money players have a reliable alternative means of funding their accounts. From time to time you do come across complaints that someone has experienced a serious delay in receiving payment for one reason or another. However, major cardrooms deal with thousands of transactions every day, and the vast majority of them do go off without a hitch.

Is the software fast, attractive, reliable and easy to use?

The quality of software for online poker can be highly variable. However, your choice could largely be a matter of personal taste. If you are unsure how to use, or whether you like, the software at a particular cardroom, then why not try a few sessions of play money poker to see how you fare with it? If you experience serious game play delays or regular server crashes then you can decide to go elsewhere without having to deposit any money on the site.

Are there any extra features such as instant hand histories, statistics and note-taking options?

Nowadays many players like to keep track of their playing statistics, while at the same time recording notes on their opponents and being able to instantly review what happened in a hand. PokerStars is one site which offer each of these facilities, whereas some other sites only offer note-taking, or just instant hand histories.

Is it safe from collusion and other forms of cheating?

Although every major site claims to have sophisticated devices in place to identify collusion or other forms of cheating, they can never be 100% reliable. Ultimately, the onus partly falls on honest players to police the games themselves. If you have justifiable suspicions about specific players at a site, report them to support – and don't play against them again in future! Remember, it is in the interests of the cardrooms to weed out the cheats, as their businesses are founded on maintaining a good reputation. If you do not have full confidence in the security of the site at which you are playing, for whatever reason, you should take your business elsewhere.

Does the site offer good freeroll events and other promotions?

Most sites run some attractive promotions from time to time, and some run good promotions nearly *all* the time. It is well worth checking out the websites of any online cardroom that you are thinking of joining to see whether they are offering a first-time deposit bonus (typically 15-25%), and what other kind of promotions they are running. Nowadays, many sites offer 'frequent player points' (or a similar scheme), whereby regular players are rewarded with benefits such as merchandise and entries to freeroll tournaments with cash prizes.

Can I beat the games they offer?

Unless you are playing purely for social reasons (or for play money), your ability to beat the games should, of course, be absolutely fundamental to your decision on where to play. To be successful in online poker in the long run you not only need an adequate bankroll and good poker skills, but also the ability to find games in which the other players are less skilful than you. The skill level of the players at a site is therefore a vital consideration in your choice of where to play.

Table 1 – Games on Offer by Site

Site	Crypto-Logic	Full Tilt	Lad-brokes	Pacific Poker	P'dise Poker	Party Poker	Poker Room	Poker Stars	Prima Poker	T'beca Poker	True Poker	Ult' Bet
Ring Games												
Hold'em (limit)	☑	☑	☑	☑	☑	☑	☑	☑	☑	☑	☑	☑
Hold'em (pot-limit)	☑	☑	☑	☑	☑	☑	☑	☑	☑	☑	☑	☑
Hold'em (no-limit)	☑	☑	☑	☑	☑	☑	☑	☑	☑	☑	☑	☑
Omaha Hi (limit)	☑	☑	☑	☒	☑	☑	☑	☑	☑	☑	☑	☑
Omaha Hi (pot-limit)	☑	☑	☑	☒	☑	☑	☑	☑	☑	☑	☑	☑
Omaha Hi/Lo (limit)	☑	☑	☑	☒	☑	☒	☑	☑	☑	☑	☑	☒
Omaha Hi/Lo (pot-limit)	☑	☑	☒	☒	☒	☒	☑	☑	☒	☒	☒	☑
Omaha Hi/Lo (no-limit)	☒	☑	☑	☑	☑	☑	☑	☒	☑	☒	☒	☑
7-Card Stud Hi (limit)	☑	☑	☒	☑	☑	☑	☑	☒	☑	☒	☒	☑
7-Card Stud Hi/Lo (limit)	☒	☒	☒	☒	☑	☒	☑	☒	☒	☒	☒	☑
Razz (limit)	☒	☒	☒	☑	☑	☒	☑	☒	☒	☒	☒	☑
5-Card Stud (limit)	☒	☒	☒	☒	☑	☒	☑	☒	☒	☒	☒	☑
5-Card Draw (limit)	☒	☒	☒	☒	☑	☒	☑	☒	☒	☒	☒	☑
Triple Draw (limit)	☒	☒	☒	☒	☒	☒	☑	☒	☒	☒	☒	☑
Crazy Pineapple (limit)	☒	☒	☒	☑	☒	☒	☒	☑	☒	☒	☒	☑
Crazy P'apple Hi/Lo (limit)	☒	☒	☒	☒	☒	☒	☒	☒	☒	☒	☒	☑
1-on-1 (dedicated tables)	☒	☒	☑	☒	☑	☒	☑	☑	☑	☑	☑	☑

Tournaments

All sites offer both single- and multi-table tournaments.

N.B. Crazy Pineapple is commonly known as three-card Irish in the UK.

Table 2 – Where to play by Game

Ring Games

Game	Site
Hold'em (limit)	All sites
Hold'em (pot-limit)	All sites
Hold'em (no-limit)	All sites
Omaha Hi (limit)	All sites
Omaha Hi (pot-limit)	All sites except Pacific Poker
Omaha Hi/Lo (limit)	All sites
Omaha Hi/Lo (pot-limit)	All sites except Pacific Poker
Omaha Hi/Lo (no-limit)	Only Full Tilt Poker and PokerStars
7-Card Stud Hi (limit)	All sites except Tribeca Tables and True Poker
7-Card Stud Hi (no-limit)	Only Ladbrokes and Prima Poker
7-Card Stud Hi (pot-limit)	Only Ladbrokes and Prima Poker
7-Card Stud Hi/Lo (limit)	All sites except CryptoLogic, Ladbrokes, Prima Poker, Tribeca Tables and True Poker
Razz (limit)	Full Tilt Poker exclusively
5-Card Stud (limit)	Only Ladbrokes, Paradise Poker and Prima Poker
5-Card Stud (pot-limit)	Only Ladbrokes and Prima Poker
5-Card Stud (no-limit)	Only Ladbrokes and Prima Poker
5-Card Draw (limit)	Only Paradise Poker and Poker Room
5-Card Draw (pot-limit)	Poker Room exclusively
Triple Draw (limit)	UltimateBet exclusively
Crazy Pineapple (limit)	Only Paradise Poker and UltimateBet
Crazy P'apple Hi/Lo (limit)	Only Paradise Poker and UltimateBet
One-on-One (heads up)	All sites except CryptoLogic, Full Tilt Poker, Pacific Poker and PartyPoker

Tournaments
All sites offer both single-table and multi-table tournaments.

Table 3 – Limit Games on Offer

Full ring games only – all stakes in dollars. Information is correct at time of writing, but subject to change.

Site	Hold'em		Omaha		Stud	
	Max	Min	Max	Min	Max	Min
CryptoLogic	150/300	0.25/0.50	20/40	0.25/0.50	20/40	1/2
Full Tilt Poker	200/400	0.25/0.50	**200/400**	0.25/0.50	**200/400**	0.25/0.50
Ladbrokes	**300/600**	0.10/0.20	**200/400**	0.12/0.25	**200/400**	0.15/0.30
Pacific Poker	30/60	0.05/0.10	30/60	0.05/0.10	15/30	0.05/0.10
Paradise Poker	40/80	0.02/0.04	10/20	0.50/1	10/20	**0.02/0.04**
PartyPoker	100/200	0.50/1	20/40	0.50/1	20/40	0.50/1
Poker Room	**300/600**	0.25/0.50	25/50	0.25/0.50	25/50	1/2
PokerStars	100/200	0.02/0.04	75/150	0.02/0.04	30/60	**0.04/0.08**
Prima Poker	100/200	0.05/0.10	50/100	0.10/0.20	50/100	0.50/1.00
Tribeca Tables	50/100	0.02/0.04	10/20	0.02/0.04	N/A	N/A
True Poker	15/30	1/2	15/30	1/2	N/A	N/A
UltimateBet	**300/600**	**0.01/0.02**	80/160	**0.01/0.02**	200/400	0.25/0.50

N.B.

1. In some instances a site will offer different limits for hi compared to hi/lo. For simplicity, this table uses the maximum range over the two games.

2. All full hold'em/Omaha/crazy pineapple games are ten-player tables (except at Full Tilt Poker and Tribeca Tables, which have nine-player tables). All other full games are eight-player tables, except for UltimateBet's triple draw, which has six-player tables, and the five-card draw games, which have five-player tables.

3. The following games are also available at different sites:

a) Ladbrokes spreads five-card stud (max $20/40; min $0.15/$0.30).

b) Paradise Poker spreads five-card draw, five-card stud, crazy pineapple hi and hi/lo (max $5/$10; min $1/$2, except five-card stud max $4/$8 and crazy pineapple hi/lo max $10/$20; min $3/$6).

c) Poker Room spreads five-card draw (max 10/20; min $1/$2).

d) Prima Poker spreads five-card stud (max $50/100; min $0.25/$0.50).

e) UltimateBet spreads crazy pineapple hi and hi/lo (max $5/$10; min $0.25/$0.50) and triple draw (max $80/$160; min $0.01/$0.02).

Table 4 – Pot-Limit and No-Limit Games on Offer

Full ring games only – all tables are listed with the maximum buy-in in dollars (hence, for example, Ladbrokes has a $20 maximum buy-in no-limit game, and then a range of games all the way up to $5,000 maximum buy-in). Information is correct at time of writing, but subject to change.

Site	No-Limit/Pot-Limit Hold'em	Pot-Limit Omaha
CryptoLogic	$30 up to $1,000	$30 up to $2,000
Full Tilt Poker	$10 up to $5,000	$10 up to $6,000
Ladbrokes	$20 up to $5,000	$30 up to $3000
Pacific Poker	$10 up to $200	N/A
Paradise Poker	**$2** up to $500	$50 up to $400
PartyPoker	$25 up to $2,000	$25 up to $2,000
Poker Room	$25 up to **$10,000**	$50 up to $200
PokerStars	$5 up to $2,000	$25 up to $2,000
Prima Poker	$10 up to **$10,000**	$10 up to **$10,000**
Tribeca Tables	$4 up to $1,000	$10 up to $400
True Poker	$25 up to $500	$25 up to $500
UltimateBet	$5 up to **$10,000**	**$5** up to $2,500

N.B.

1. In some instances a site will offer different limits for no-limit compared to pot-limit or Omaha hi compared to hi/lo. For simplicity, this table uses the maximum range over the two games.

2. All full hold'em and Omaha games are ten-player tables, except at Full Tilt Poker and Tribeca Tables, which have nine-player tables.

3. In nearly all cases the maximum buy-ins for these games is 100 times the big blind. Thus a $400 maximum buy-in game would have blinds of $2 and $4.

4. The minimum buy-in is typically 20% of the maximum buy-in. Thus a $400 maximum buy-in game would normally have a minimum buy-in of $80.

5. The following games are also available at different sites:

a) Full Tilt Poker and PokerStars also spread no-limit Omaha hi/lo.

b) Ladbrokes and Prima Poker also spread pot-limit and no-limit seven- and five-card stud.

c) Poker Room also spreads pot-limit five-card draw.

Table 5 – Maximum Rakes

Nearly all online cardrooms run a 'no flop, no drop' policy, whereby no rake is taken if the hand ends before the flop. The rake is typically 5% (e.g. $0.25 is taken when the pot reaches $5.00) with the maximums outlined below. In Table 6 I have supplied a recommended rake structure for the purposes of comparison. Information is correct at time of writing, but subject to change.

High, Middle and Low-Limit
All sites: $2/$4 & above (& pot-limit/no-limit) – max $3
However, Tribeca Tables has a maximum $4 rake on its $30/$60 and $50/$100 games.

Micro-Limit
$1/$2 & below – max $3 (Ladbrokes/True Poker/CryptoLogic)
$1/$2 & below – max $1.50 (Poker Room/Prima Poker)
$1/$2 & below – max $1 (others)
UltimateBet does not rake its $0.01/$0.02 games and Tribeca Tables does not rake its $0.02/$0.04 games. Also both the $0.02/$0.04 and $0.04/$0.08 games at PokerStars are rake-free, as are the $0.02/$0.04 and $0.05/$0.10 games at Paradise Poker. Most other super-micro-limit games are raked.

One-on-One
Max $3 (Ladbrokes)
Max $2 (CryptoLogic)
Max $1 (PokerStars/PartyPoker/Prima Poker/True Poker/Poker Room/Pacific Poker/Tribeca Tables)
Max $0.50 (Full Tilt Poker/Paradise Poker – dedicated heads-up tables only/UltimateBet)

No-Limit and Pot-Limit
All sites – max $3

N.B.

1. CryptoLogic, Full Tilt Poker, Pacific Poker and PartyPoker do not have dedicated heads-up 'ring game' tables.

2. At Ladbrokes, Pacific Poker, PartyPoker, Poker Room, PokerStars, Prima Poker, Tribeca Tables and True Poker the maximum $1.00 rake also applies to three-handed games. Full Tilt Poker and Paradise Poker also have a maximum $1.00 rake on three-player games.

3. At UltimateBet the maximum $0.50 rake also applies to three-handed games. At Tribeca Tables a maximum $0.50 rake applies to three-handed games of $1/$2 and below.

Table 6 – Recommended Rake Structures

The following tables list what could be regarded as standard rakes for different cash games. In many cases, the major cardrooms do not actually meet these standards (although in a few rare instances they do actually exceed them).

No rake should be taken on limit games of $0.04/$0.08 and below.

Limit games up to $1/$2

Number of players	$5 Pot	$10 Pot	$15 Pot	$20 Pot	Max Rake
2	$0.25	$0.25			$0.50
3-10	$0.25	$0.25	$0.25	$0.25	$1.00

Limit games from $2/$4 to $10/$20

Number of players	$20 Pot	$40 Pot	$60 Pot	Max Rake
2	$0.50			$0.50
3	$0.50	$0.50		$1.00
4-5	$1.00	$1.00		$2.00
6-10	$1.00	$1.00	$1.00	$3.00

Limit games from $15/30 upwards

Number of players	$40 Pot	$70 Pot	$100 Pot	Max Rake
2	$0.50			$0.50
3	$1.00			$1.00
4-5	$1.00	$1.00		$2.00
6-10	$1.00	$1.00	$1.00	$3.00

No-limit and pot-limit games

$0.05 per $1.00 in the pot up to a maximum of $0.50 for 2-3 players, $2.00 for 4-5 players and $3.00 for 6-10 players.

Online Cardroom Reviews

The following section includes reviews of 12 of the most popular, well-established online cardrooms and networks: CryptoLogic, Full Tilt Poker, Ladbrokes, Pacific Poker, Paradise Poker, PartyPoker, Poker Room, PokerStars, Prima Poker, Tribeca Tables, True Poker and UltimateBet. Each site is discussed in some detail and then given an assessment based on the following criteria:

1. Software and Graphics

2. Game Variety – Ring Games

3. Game Variety – Tournaments

4. Site Traffic

5. Customer Support

6. Rakes and Tournament Registration Fees

7. Promotions and Special Events

8. Website

An overall rating is then awarded to each site.

The online poker business has exploded in the past few years, and new sites are being launched every few weeks. Indeed, there are now over 250 online cardrooms and skins! The final part of this section discusses some of these other sites.

PokerStars

Slogan: 'Where poker players become world champions'

URL: http://www.pokerstars.com/

Location: Costa Rica (licensed and regulated by the Kahnawake Gaming Commission in Canada)

Launched: December 2001 (for real money games)

Transaction methods: VISA, MasterCard, NETeller, FirePay and Central Coin

Special Features

♠ Organisers of the World Championship of Online Poker
♠ Facility to upload an image to place next to your chair

Hits

♠ Fast, reliable software
♠ Very popular single- and multi-table tournaments
♠ Frequent player points scheme

- ♠ Rake-free super-micro-limit tables
- ♠ Excellent e-mail support
- ♠ Lobby information includes players/flop and hands/hour
- ♠ Good note-taking and statistics functions

Misses

- ♠ No telephone support
- ♠ No buddy list
- ♠ Arguably tougher opposition than most online sites

Review

Introduction

In a very short space of time PokerStars has emerged from being a start-up company to become one of the most popular online cardrooms, with several hundred thousand real money clients. This has been achieved largely through developing great software and providing excellent multi-table tournaments. In addition, PokerStars has shown itself to be highly responsive to customer needs, even making software changes and organising special promotional tournaments in direct response to feedback suggestions from clients.

PokerStars' main claim to fame is the fact that it supplied the winner of the main event at both the 2003 and 2004 World Series of Poker. In 2003 Chris Moneymaker (an accountant from Tennessee) turned a $39 PokerStars satellite entry fee into $2.5 million, and in 2004 patent attorney Greg Raymer converted a $160 satellite into $5 million, defeating over 2,500 players in the process. Indeed, the 2004 runner-up, David Williams, also won his $10,000 seat in a PokerStars satellite. PokerStars VP of Marketing Dan Goldman stated: 'While PokerStars qualifiers represented only 12% of the players in the World Series of Poker, they collectively took home over 40% of the total prize money awarded. We had 28 players finish in the money for a total of almost $11 million in prize money. Four of the top nine finishers in the event qualified on our site.'

In 2002 PokerStars organised the first World Championship of Online Poker (WCOOP), with a total prize fund of $800,000, spread across nine events in a week-long festival. Since then the WCOOP has become established as one of the world's leading online poker events. There were 12 events in the 2004 edition, and the first prize in the $2,500 buy-in main event was a staggering $424,945, with a total prize pool of over $2 million. In the months leading up WCOOP, PokerStars organises dozens of satellite qualification events, with buy-ins from as little as $10 in addition to frequent player points satellites.

In 2004 the site also began hosting its own live-action event, the Poker-Stars Caribbean Adventure, on the World Poker Tour, which has been such a huge hit for the Travel Channel in the US. In 2004-05 Poker-Stars also sponsored the first ever European Poker Tour, which included events in Barcelona, London, Copenhagen and Dublin, culminating in a grand final in Monte Carlo. These events were subsequently broadcast across Europe on Eurosport TV. Naturally, PokerStars has been very active in running online satellites for both the WPT and EPT.

Since early 2003 well-known author and 1983 WSOP Championship event winner Tom McEvoy has been a member of the PokerStars team. Apart from making regular appearances in cash games, he takes part in various promotions for PokerStars. For example, the top overall PokerStars tournament player each week currently qualifies to face him heads-up for a $2000 prize, which rolls over to the following week if the challenger is unsuccessful.

In May 2003, PokerStars submitted extensive information about its random number generator to two independent organisations, Cigital and BMM International. These companies were given full access to the source code and were able to confirm the randomness and security of the shuffle. Cigital has also undertaken extensive stress-testing on the software, to ensure that it can stand up to tens of thousands of users.

In addition, PokerStars has taken steps to ensure that players' funds are completely protected. All player deposits are kept in segregated accounts held by the Royal Bank of Scotland.

Software and Graphics

The undoubted jewel in the PokerStars crown is its powerful multi-table tournament software, which has always been the envy of other cardrooms. This software is robust and flexible enough to handle tournaments ranging from a handful of players through to many thousands. The software seamlessly manages the players and tables in such a way that as every additional player is eliminated, the remaining players are evenly balanced across the remaining tables, until ultimately one final table of nine players remains. At the same time every remaining player is able to keep track of exactly where they stand in the event by accessing the 'Info' facility, and can also see which other players are still in the competition by checking the tournament lobby. One innovative feature of the tournament software is the 'Time Bank', which enables players to take extra time on any critical decisions that they may face. However, each player only receives a set time for each event; once their Time Bank has expired they must act in the normal allotted time period or else their hand will be folded.

Another innovation that PokerStars brought into the game was the facility to not only store notes on your opponents, but also to keep track of your playing statistics (an idea that was quickly picked up by Paradise Poker and other sites).

The PokerStars lobby is one of the most comprehensive, providing information on the average players per flop and average pot size, together with the number of hands dealt per hour. PokerStars hand histories can either be e-mailed in the traditional way, or viewed instantly by opening the new 'Instant Hand History' program.

At PokerStars you also have the facility to upload an image to set at your place at the table. However, whilst this option is quite fun, some regular players prefer to play with these images switched off so as not to clutter the screen.

PokerStars does not use (and has never used) prop players. You are permitted to play up to five tables at a time.

Game Variety

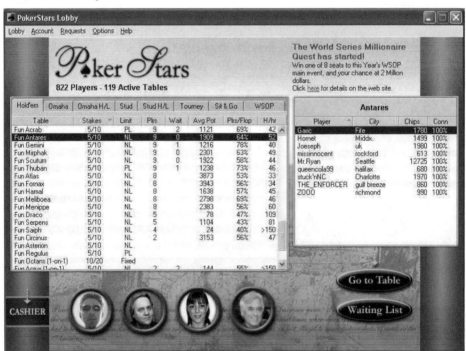

PokerStars spreads the standard choice of games: hold'em, Omaha (both hi and hi/lo) and seven-card stud (both hi and hi/lo). All of these games are available both in ring game and tournament format. In addition, PokerStars is one of only two major sites to offer a no-limit Omaha hi/lo game.

The biggest game at PokerStars is currently $100/$200 limit hold'em, a game which is restricted to approved players (as is the $75/$150 limit Omaha hi/lo game). Only those who have been specifically vetted by the site are permitted to take a seat in these games. In this way, PokerStars is better able to police its high-limit games and prevent collusion.

In early 2003 PokerStars adopted a clever marketing ploy to attract newcomers to poker to the site – the first super-micro-limit online tables: $0.02/$0.04 limit hold'em/Omaha and $0.04/$0.08 seven-card stud games with no rake, an innovation that has been quickly copied by some other sites. PokerStars was also the first major site to introduce 'high-speed' tables, at which blinds are posted automatically and the players have less time in which to act.

At the end of 2002 PokerStars added sit and go tournaments to its already very popular range of tournaments. These events, with longer 10-minute (rather than 10-hand) increases in the blinds and 1,500 starting chips (instead of 800 or 1,000) offer more play compared to most other sites and are extremely popular.

Site Traffic

For reasons outlined above, tournament traffic far outweighs ring game traffic at PokerStars. However, as a result of some innovative ideas, ring game traffic is much higher now than at anytime in the past. In early 2003 the daily peak was typically somewhere in excess of 300 cash game players with a further 750 or so players competing in tournaments. By 2005 these figures had increased exponentially, with peaks of well over 5,000 cash game players and 27,000 tournament players. In fact, PokerStars is currently the second most popular site for both cash games and tournaments.

It is worth noting that PokerStars has a larger proportion of European clients than either Paradise Poker or PartyPoker, which means that its busiest period falls a little earlier in the day.

Customer Support

Although it does not have live hosts (except for big buy-in tournament final tables etc.) or telephone support, PokerStars provides an extremely efficient e-mail support service.

Rakes and Tournament Registration Fees

The rake at PokerStars is fairly industry-standard. There are no dedicated one-on-one ring game tables, and the heads-up rake carries a fairly expensive $1 cap.

Standard weekly tournament buy-ins range from freerolls (held daily) and $1 events with no drop, through to $300 events with a $20 entry fee. Satellites are available for the big weekly events. The site also runs heads-up two-player tournaments, for which the registration fee is only 5% of the buy-in (and even less for bigger buy-in events).

Promotions and Special Events

PokerStars has some of the best online poker promotions. In its regular player reward scheme, one Frequent Player Point (FPP) is awarded for each raked hand and five points for each $1 levied in tournament registration fees. These FPPs can be redeemed for goods or for entries into designated weekly, monthly and special tournaments.

The highlight of the wide-ranging PokerStars weekly tournament schedule is its big Sunday night events. Currently these are $200 (& $15) buy-in with a guaranteed prize fund of $500,000, with a larger $500 (& $30) buy-in for the last Sunday of the month, with a $700,000 guarantee. In February 2005 entries for the $200 event surpassed 2,500 for the first time.

Furthermore, PokerStars sometimes adds considerable sums to its prize pools. For example, in October 2002 PokerStars organised the largest online tournament to that date, a $1 buy-in no-limit hold'em event, for which they added $1,500 to the prize fund. It easily filled its maximum quota of 1,000 players, 27 of whom received prizes! The very next week PokerStars broke their own record with a 1,500-player, $3 entry fee, $5500-added competition which attracted players from more than 30 countries. First prize was $2,750, a very reasonable return on $3!

Then, as part of its first anniversary celebrations PokerStars in December 2002, ran a special 1,500-player, $10 buy-in no-limit hold'em event, for which they guaranteed a $25,000 prize fund. In the event, 1,394 players actually took part, so in effect the sponsorship for this tournament alone amounted to over $11,000!

Website

There is always something new happening at PokerStars, and their website reflects this. The home page is updated regularly with the latest news and developments, and there is a very useful site map to help you find what your way around. In April 2005 PokerStars even introduced its very own blog!

Rating

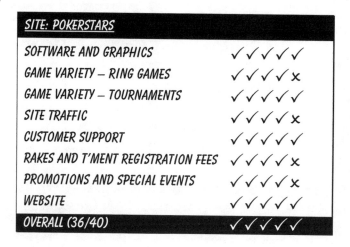

SITE: POKERSTARS	
SOFTWARE AND GRAPHICS	✓ ✓ ✓ ✓ ✓
GAME VARIETY – RING GAMES	✓ ✓ ✓ ✓ ✗
GAME VARIETY – TOURNAMENTS	✓ ✓ ✓ ✓ ✓
SITE TRAFFIC	✓ ✓ ✓ ✓ ✗
CUSTOMER SUPPORT	✓ ✓ ✓ ✓ ✓
RAKES AND T'MENT REGISTRATION FEES	✓ ✓ ✓ ✓ ✗
PROMOTIONS AND SPECIAL EVENTS	✓ ✓ ✓ ✓ ✗
WEBSITE	✓ ✓ ✓ ✓ ✓
OVERALL (36/40)	✓ ✓ ✓ ✓ ✓

UltimateBet

Courtesy of UltimateBet.com Copyright © 2003

Slogan: 'Where virtually everyone plays poker™'

URL: **http://www.ultimatebet.com/**

Location: Antigua (licensed and regulated by the Kahnawake Gaming Commission in Canada)

Launched: May 2001 (for real money games)

Transaction methods: VISA, MasterCard, NETeller, FirePay, Citadel (US only), SFPay (US only), bank draft and cashier's cheque

Special Features

♠ Unique MiniView™ feature
♠ Wide selection of different games, including five-card stud, five-card draw and crazy pineapple

♠ 'Team Ultimate Bet', featuring well-known champions and other poker figures

♠ UltimateBuddy™ buddy list

Hits

♠ Very fast software

♠ High-limit games

♠ Rake-free super-micro-limit tables

♠ Frequent players points scheme

♠ Lobby information includes players/flop and hands/hour

Misses

♠ No telephone support

Review

Introduction

When UltimateBet launched back in 2001, it seemed inevitable that, with attractive-looking software and the active participation of such poker celebrities as Phil Hellmuth, Annie Duke and Dave 'Devilfish' Ulliott, it would not be long before the site emerged as a serious challenger to the market leaders. However, although UltimateBet has established a firm place as one of the top half-dozen or so sites in terms of traffic, it has never become a serious rival for the No.1 spot. Although in the early days this could be attributed to Paradise Poker's 'early start' advantage, this is by no means the whole story. After all, both PartyPoker and PokerStars, which were launched even later than UltimateBet, have a much wider player base nowadays.

It is interesting to speculate why the UltimateBet launch was not as successful as many people predicted. Firstly, when the site was initially launched, its software was not as fast as players were used to at Paradise Poker, so some potential clients found the games relatively tedious by comparison. Undoubtedly, another contributing factor was the high rakes on low-limit games that it charged at the time. Although the rake caps themselves were adjusted in line with the industry standard in February 2002, UltimateBet has always extracted the rake for its $4/$8 (and below) games at more frequent intervals than, for example, Paradise Poker and PokerStars, which can add up to a considerable extra charge per player over time. If UltimateBet had taken the opposite approach and gone straight after the low-limit market with a lower than standard rake, then perhaps it would have established a larger market share from the outset.

In July 2002 UltimateBet tried to bolster its client base with a scheme known as UB-2. The basic idea was that players who signed up to play at the site via UB-2 would receive a rake rebate after they had played a certain number of hours per month. Members of UB-2 would also be rewarded both for referring new members and for any additional members whom that player in turn brought to the site. However, to many people this seemed like a classic 'pyramid' marketing scheme and it was widely criticised, with the result it was quickly discontinued, having done little to help UltimateBet's credibility in the fledgling online poker industry.

Software and Graphics

Courtesy of UltimateBet.com Copyright © 2003

The UltimateBet software runs quickly and smoothly with a quite individual-looking, clean, stream-lined interface. Indeed, in my opinion the cash games at this site are currently the fastest anywhere. One very attractive feature is the unique MiniView™ feature, which allows users to play at a table not much bigger than a banner ad if they so wish, thereby leaving the rest of their screen real estate free for other things. Naturally the MiniView™ feature lends itself perfectly to players who like to play more than one table at once.

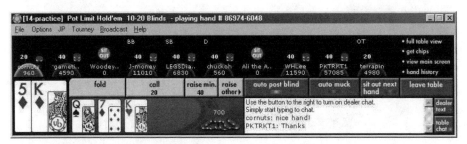

Courtesy of UltimateBet.com Copyright © 2003

UltimateBet's clients also have the option of being able to see when and where their friends and other favourite players are playing on the site (and keep notes on them) through a new free program, Ultimate-Buddy™, which is available for download at UltimateBuddy.com.

Game Variety

The range of games on offer at UltimateBet is one of the widest in the industry, with the full selection of hold'em, Omaha and seven-card stud games together with some interesting wrinkles. In addition, until Paradise Poker added a selection of new games in November 2002, UltimateBet was the only site to offer crazy pineapple. And in fact it is currently the only major site to offer triple draw (in both ace to five and deuce to seven versions). There is a fair amount of high-limit action on the site and players are permitted to play up to three tables at a time.

The site runs very popular single-table and multi-table tournaments. Indeed, the multi-table events have a very slow blind structure, which provides competitors with plenty of time to play (especially in the larger buy-in events, in which the players have bigger starting stacks). There are tournaments for all budgets – indeed the site starts a new tournament on the hour, every hour (24/7).

Courtesy of UltimateBet.com Copyright © 2003

Site Traffic

UltimateBet is a very popular site. There are usually around 2,500 ring game players at peak times, with another 4,000 or so competing in either single- or multi-table tournaments.

Customer Support

The site does not offer live hosts or telephone support, only e-mail support, which is much more reliable nowadays than it used to be.

Rakes and Tournament Registration Fees

Although the rake caps at UltimateBet are comparable with those at other sites, there are a couple of key differences for low-limit players. First, the drop is taken at more frequent intervals for $4/$8 games and below than at some other sites, which obviously makes it more expensive. However, to partially offset this, the maximum rake for short-handed games at $2/$4 and $3/$6 is only $1.50 compared to the usual $2.00 elsewhere. Furthermore, the rake structure for the higher limit games is very player-friendly. Additionally, the rake for heads-up and three-player tables at UltimateBet is extremely competitive, capped at $0.50.

Tournament buys-in range from $1 to $5,000 for single-table events and $1 to $200 for regular weekly multi-table events. There is no drop for the $1 multi-table events, and a 10% drop for other events below $100 (the site's $5 events only carry a $0.50 charge compared to the usual $1 elsewhere). The $5 heads-up no-limit matches are also good value, with only a $0.25 charge for each player. There are also numerous freeroll tournaments. One notable feature of UltimateBet multi-table tournaments is that they occasionally place a 'bounty' on a particular player — the client who eliminates the designated bounty player qualifies for a special prize!

Promotions and Special Events

UltimateBet has its own group of well-known faces (known as 'Team UltimateBet') which comprises Phil Hellmuth, Annie Duke, Dave 'Devilfish' Ulliott and Antonio Esfandiari. These team members make regular appearances at the site, enabling you to play against stars of the poker world at quite low limits (as little as $3/$6). Annie Duke, in particular, is almost always willing to offer advice on how you should have played a hand if you ask her!

UltimateBet runs a frequent player reward scheme, whereby players are awarded points for every raked game or tournament they play, with extra points for players who start up new games. These Ultimate Points™ can then be converted into merchandise purchases or entries to various tournaments. There are also regular reload bonuses.

In January 2004 UltimateBet organised the first-ever million guaranteed online tournament, known as 'The Stone Cold Nuts'. This was a huge success, attracting over 700 players and boasting an eventual first prize over $350,000.

UltimateBet's flagship event is the multi-million dollar Aruba Classic, which is held in September each year as part of the World Poker Tour (in fact, UltimateBet was one of the charter members of the WPT). Satellites for the Aruba Classic start in February.

Website

One excellent feature of the UltimateBet website is an interactive tu-

tutorial for first-time users. Apart from the usual help information and details of current promotions, the website also has a Team UltimateBet section, which contains biographical profiles of the celebrities who endorse the site, together with some interesting articles which they have contributed. Poker writer John Vorhaus contributes regular articles, and also supplies a blog from the some of the big tournaments.

Rating

SITE: ULTIMATEBET	
SOFTWARE AND GRAPHICS	✓ ✓ ✓ ✓ ✗
GAME VARIETY – RING GAMES	✓ ✓ ✓ ✓ ✓
GAME VARIETY – TOURNAMENTS	✓ ✓ ✓ ✓ ✓
SITE TRAFFIC	✓ ✓ ✓ ✓ ✗
CUSTOMER SUPPORT	✓ ✓ ✓ ✓ ✗
RAKES AND T'MENT REGISTRATION FEES	✓ ✓ ✓ ✓ ✗
PROMOTIONS AND SPECIAL EVENTS	✓ ✓ ✓ ✓ ✗
WEBSITE	✓ ✓ ✓ ✓ ✗
OVERALL (34/40)	✓ ✓ ✓ ✓ ✗

Paradise Poker

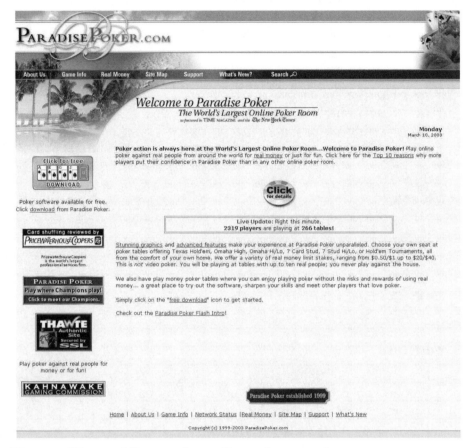

Slogan: 'The world's premier online poker room'

URL: **http://www.paradisepoker.com/**

Location: Costa Rica (licensed and regulated by the Kahnawake Gaming Commission in Canada)

Launched: September 1999 (for real money games)

Transaction methods: VISA, MasterCard, NETeller, FirePay and Switch/Maestro

Special Features

♠ One of the market leaders since 1999
♠ Wide selection of different games, including five-card stud, five-card draw and crazy pineapple

Hits

♠ Fast, reliable software
♠ Good e-mail customer support
♠ Rake-free super-micro-limit tables
♠ Lobby information includes players/flop and hands/hour
♠ Good note-taking and statistics functions

Misses

♠ No telephone support
♠ No frequent player points scheme
♠ Expensive tournament registration fees
♠ No instant hand history facility
♠ No buddy list

Review

Introduction

Despite a number of challenges over the past few years, Paradise Poker has managed to retain its long-standing position as one of the online poker market leaders. With a huge client base, it is popular with players from all over the world, breaking down time-zone barriers with constant action round the clock.

In October 2004 Paradise was bought out by the large UK-based sports book, Sportingbet plc, a publicly-traded company on the London Stock Exchange, for around $300 million. Sportingbet's share price has more than tripled since then.

A browse through the archives from a few years ago at rec.gambling.poker or any other poker forum is sure to reveal more accusations of collusion or cheating at Paradise Poker than any other site. However, given that Paradise Poker held the largest market share for several years, this is not in itself any particular cause for concern. It is undoubtedly true that in, the early years of online poker, more players lost money at Paradise Poker than at any other site, but this is hardly surprising because so many more players had actually played at Paradise Poker than anywhere else! And as we have already discussed in the section on 'Cheating', many players who believe they may have been cheated are actually quite mistaken.

Software and Graphics

The Paradise Poker interface is exceptionally clean, and the software generally runs smoothly and quickly (though you may wish to experiment with deselecting 'enable animation' and selecting 'optimise graphics', which may possibly speed it up even more). When the first edition of this book was published, I had one minor gripe – the precise pot size was not provided numerically on screen unless you ran your cursor over the pot (most other sites provided this information numerically somewhere on the table). However, I am pleased to see that Paradise Poker has since taken this criticism on board, and the pot size is now clearly displayed above the dealer's tray.

Paradise Poker was the first site to offer the facility to play two tables at once, though as we have seen, this can be something of a mixed blessing for most players. However, unlike some sites, Paradise Poker does not allow players to play at more than three tables at once. This does have the advantage that the games are not slowed down by players who are busy on a handful of other tables, but on the other hand there is nothing to prevent such players from playing additional tables at another site. To prevent all-in abuse, there is no all-in protection at Paradise Poker. Once you are timed out, your hand is folded.

In 2002 Paradise Poker belatedly introduced both notes and statistics functions for its players, following the lead taken by PokerStars in this regard. However, unlike its major rivals, Paradise Poker does not currently provide any facility for viewing hand histories instantly, just the standard e-mail facility.

Game Variety

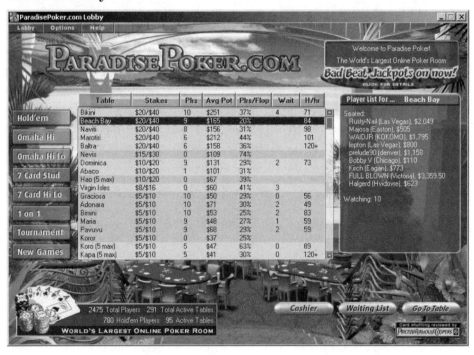

Along with UltimateBet, Paradise Poker leads the industry in the variety of ring games on offer. Apart from the standard hold'em, Omaha and seven-card stud games, Paradise Poker also has five-card stud, five-card draw and crazy pineapple hi (commonly known as three-card Irish in the UK) and hi/lo. Unusually, the short-handed tables are five players maximum rather than six maximum.

Although the site had single-table tournaments from as far back as September 2000, Paradise Poker was a relative late-comer in the field of multi-table tournaments, which were not launched until December 2003. However, there is now a full range of multi-table events for hold'em, Omaha and seven-card stud.

Site Traffic

Almost since it was launched, Paradise Poker has been one of the most popular online sites for ring games. At peak times there are typically over 2,000 players playing in cash games, with another 4,000 or so in tournaments Even at off-peak times there are always over 500 ring game money players at the Paradise Poker tables. The increase in online competition since 2001 has inevitably led to a loss of some of Paradise Poker's relative market share, but its total player base is as strong as ever.

Customer Support

Although the Paradise Poker customer support is exclusively e-mail based, it has an excellent reputation and generally responds promptly to any enquiries.

Rakes and Tournament Registration Fees

Paradise Poker offers an attractive rake on its $15/$30, $20/$40 and $40/$80 games: $1 once the pot reaches $40, another $1 when the pot gets to $70 and a further $1 when the pot tops $100. Furthermore, the super-micro-limit games, up to and including $0.05/$0.10, are not raked.

On the surface Paradise Poker's 9% fee on gross tournament buy-in seems fairly attractive. In fact, however, this makes re-buy and add-on events extremely expensive for the players, since they have to pay a 9% fee on *each additional* buy-in. Furthermore, most other sites do actually take less than 9% for their bigger buy-in tournaments (i.e. buy-ins in excess of $100).

The buy-ins for Paradise Poker's single-table tournaments range from $5 to $300. The $1 charge levied on the $5 buy-in events represents poor value for players, but the 10% drop for their other single-table tournaments is standard for online events. (Paradise Poker also charges only $9 for the $100 buy-in events and $25 for the $300 buy-in events.)

Promotions and Special Events

Since August 2004 Paradise Poker has had a flagship $100,000 guaranteed tournament every Sunday night, for which the buy-in is $300 (satellites are available). From time to time Paradise Poker runs special promotions, but it does not have a frequent players points programme. There is currently a 25% bonus on first-time deposits.

In July 2005 Paradise Poker launched the world's first-ever million-dollar freeroll, a promotion which culminated in ten players meeting face-to-face to contest a $1 million first prize.

Website

The Paradise Poker website is well structured, with a search engine to help clients find what they are looking for. However, historically, the site has not been updated very often. This lack of fresh content meant that unless you have a specific question in mind, it would be unlikely that you would be inclined to return to the website on a regular basis. To partially combat this, in June 2005 Paradise Poker followed the example of PokerStars by introducing its very own blog.

Rating

SITE: PARADISE POKER	
SOFTWARE AND GRAPHICS	✓ ✓ ✓ ✓ ✓
GAME VARIETY – RING GAMES	✓ ✓ ✓ ✓ ✓
GAME VARIETY – TOURNAMENTS	✓ ✓ ✓ ✓ ✗
SITE TRAFFIC	✓ ✓ ✓ ✓ ✗
CUSTOMER SUPPORT	✓ ✓ ✓ ✓ ✓
RAKES AND T'MENT REGISTRATION FEES	✓ ✓ ✗ ✗ ✗
PROMOTIONS AND SPECIAL EVENTS	✓ ✓ ✓ ✗ ✗
WEBSITE	✓ ✓ ✓ ✓ ✗
OVERALL (32/40)	✓ ✓ ✓ ✓ ✗

PartyPoker

Slogan: 'Welcome to the world's largest poker room!'

URL: **http://www.partypoker.com/**

Location: Gibraltar (licensed and regulated by the Government of Gibraltar)

Launched: August 2001 (for real money games)

Transaction methods: VISA, MasterCard, NETeller, FirePay (US only), Switch/Maestro, Western Union, Citadel (US only), iGM-Pay (US only), FPS-ePassport, wire transfer

Special Features

- ♠ Organisers of PartyPoker.com Million tournament
- ♠ Buddy list
- ♠ Designated high hand and bad beat jackpot tables

Hits

- ♠ Currently by far the biggest site
- ♠ Toll-free 24-hour support number
- ♠ Great promotions, based on frequent play
- ♠ Hosted by highly respected Mike Sexton

Misses

- ♠ No lobby information on players/flop or hands/hour
- ♠ Very limited statistics functions
- ♠ Hit-or-miss Indian-based support centre

Review

Introduction

Since it launched in 2001, PartyPoker has taken online poker by storm. Using its own custom-built software, supported by a major affiliate scheme, and backed up by a powerful marketing campaign based primarily around the PartyPoker.com Million, PartyPoker immediately carved out a strong niche for itself. By 2003 it had already bypassed long-term market leader Paradise Poker to become the undisputed No.1 in terms of site traffic. And since then it has gone from strength to strength, dedicating huge resources to marketing itself to the general public.

PartyPoker is hosted by the highly respected Mike Sexton, the 1989 WSOP Seven-Card Stud Eight or Better Champion and winner of numerous other major titles, who is better known to most people as commentator on the World Poker Tour. Mike Sexton founded the Tournament of Champions of Poker and is regarded as one of the world's leading ambassadors of the game. He joined PartyPoker as host/consultant in 2001 and is credited as being the creator of the PartyPoker.com Million.

Another interesting aspect of PartyPoker is that it has other several doorways (or 'skins') at multipoker.com, pokernow.com, coralpoker.com, eurobetpoker.com, intertopspoker.com and empirepoker.com. Clients of Empire Poker (for example) play on the same software, against exactly the same opponents (and receiving the same customer support) as those of PartyPoker. However, the two companies are independently owned and marketed. It is permissible to hold a separate account with each, using different handles (though not to play simultaneously using both accounts).

In June 2005 PartyGaming (owners of PartyPoker, Starluck Casino and PartyBingo) launched on the London Stock Exchange with an initial market value of well over $8 billion. This was the biggest London flotation in the past five years. On the back of PartyGaming's astonishing first quarter operating profit of $128 million, the initial share offer was over-subscribed three times over.

Software and Graphics

When it was launched, the PartyPoker software came under fire for being quite slow and clunky, and although most of the problems were eradicated when the software was given a major upgrade in June 2002, it is still perhaps not as smooth as it could be. Many aspects of the software are still somewhat inferior to those of its main competitors.

PartyPoker permits its clients to play up to four tables at the same time. Although the lobby lists the average pot size over the last 20 hands, no information on the average number of players per flop or number of hands per hour is provided. Furthermore, unlike its main rivals, PartyPoker does not currently offer its clients much statistical feedback on their own play, although it does have a note-taking facility (simply right-click on a player's name at the table and select 'Player Notes'). You can also find out when your friends (or 'fish') are online by using the Buddy List under 'My Account' in the menus at the top of the lobby.

In the past couple of years PartyPoker has developed its hand history software so that players can view their histories without having to request an e-mail. In addition, all hand histories are automatically logged in a folder in your computer, from where they can be viewed at a later date (or imported into a poker-tracking software program).

Game Variety

PartyPoker offers the standard choice of games: hold'em, Omaha (both hi and hi/lo) and seven-card stud (both hi and hi/lo). There are currently no one-on-one tables at PartyPoker, but there are six-player maximum tables for short-handed games (and also some nine-handed $10/$20 and $1/$2 games). Players are permitted to play up to four tables at a time.

Both the single- and multi-table tournaments are very popular, and the site has recently adopted two PokerStars concepts: a 'Time Bank' to allow players more time for critical decisions, and sit and go multi-table tournaments.

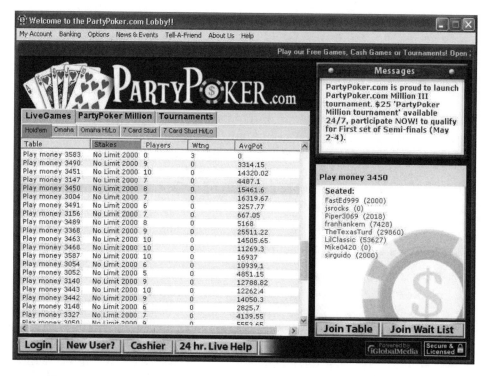

Site Traffic

PartyPoker is currently by far the most popular site. At peak times there are typically somewhere around 17,000 ring game money players on the site, with another 25,000-30,000 competing in either single- or multi-table tournaments.

Customer Support

Although PartyPoker does offer 24/7 toll-free telephone support, its overall support system is below standard. The support centre is based in India, and some of their staff do not have a full grasp of English (let alone poker!). This means that obtaining satisfactory responses is a rather a hit-or-miss affair.

Rakes and Tournament Registration Fees

Unlike most other sites, PartyPoker rakes in increments of $0.50 rather than of $1 for games of $2/$4 and above. This adds up to a considerable additional rake expense for regular players over time. Furthermore, the rake structure is less attractive for lower-limit players, since the site charges a $0.50 rake when the pot reaches $5 in $0.50/$1 and $1/$2 limit games, whereas at most other sites the rake does not reach $0.50 until the pot tops $10. The one advantage that Party has over other sites is that the six-maximum tables are capped at a $2 rake.

PartyPoker regular weekly tournament buy-ins range from $5 through to $200. There is an expensive $1 charge for the $5 tourneys. The buy-in for the fifth PartyPoker.com Million was $31 (plus a $3 fee) with each single-table (10-player) event winner qualifying for the semi-finals. Each semi-finalist then had a shot at winning a holiday for two on the PartyPoker Million cruise (and a paid entry into the final and the opportunity to perhaps take down the big prize).

Promotions and Special Events

PartyPoker is undoubtedly *the* leading player in the field of online poker marketing promotions. In addition to the huge first prize in the flagship annual PartyPoker.com Million (see below), PartyPoker also offers its regular players various other perks (such as frequent reload bonuses), which are typically linked to the number of raked hands in which that player has participated. PartyPoker also actively encourages its clients to refer their friends to the site, offering a referral bonus to both the referring player and the friend.

PartyPoker also has special designated high hand and bad beat jackpot tables. In January 2005 the bad beat jackpot hit a record of $739,621, with the 'loser' of the hand netting an amazing $268,867.54.

After six months of online satellites, the first PartyPoker.com Million final took place on the cruise ship 'Elation' on the Mexican Riviera in March 2002. Televised by the Travel Channel in the US, it boasted the largest-ever prize pool in the history of limit hold'em and was also remarkable in two other respects. First, it was won by Californian professional tournament player Kathy Liebert, marking the first time that a woman had captured a poker title of such magnitude, and second, the runner-up was novice Berj Kacherian from Los Angeles, competing in his first-ever poker tournament, who was one of 100 qualifiers from the PartyPoker online satellite series. Kathy took home the million dollars, and Berj made a very respectable return of $93,600 on his original $22 investment! In 2003 the PartyPoker.com

Million became part of the fledgling World Poker Tour, since when it has gone from strength to strength.

Website

PartyPoker offers some of the most exciting promotions in the industry, and its website is a good place to find out more about them. You can also log in to the site to find out the current status of your deposit bonuses, to make deposits or to transfer funds to a friend's account. The PartyPoker website also has a search engine and a useful site map, although it is buried under 24hr. help and therefore not easy to find! However, the site currently lags behind its major rivals in one key area: there is very little topical content such as strategy articles and blogs.

Rating

SITE: PARTYPOKER	
SOFTWARE AND GRAPHICS	✓ ✓ ✓ ✓ ✗
GAME VARIETY – RING GAMES	✓ ✓ ✓ ✓ ✗
GAME VARIETY – TOURNAMENTS	✓ ✓ ✓ ✓ ✓
SITE TRAFFIC	✓ ✓ ✓ ✓ ✓
CUSTOMER SUPPORT	✓ ✓ ✗ ✗ ✗
RAKES AND T'MENT REGISTRATION FEES	✓ ✓ ✗ ✗ ✗
PROMOTIONS AND SPECIAL EVENTS	✓ ✓ ✓ ✓ ✓
WEBSITE	✓ ✓ ✓ ✓ ✗
OVERALL (31/40)	✓ ✓ ✓ ✓ ✗

Full Tilt Poker

Slogan: 'There's a new game in town. Are you in?'

URL: **http://www.fulltiltpoker.com/**

Location: Aruba (licensed and regulated by the Kahnawake Gaming Commission in Canada)

Launched: 2004

Transaction methods: VISA, MasterCard, NETeller, FirePay (US only) and ePassporte.

Special Features

- ♠ Endorsed by a team of world-famous professionals
- ♠ Select from a range of avatars to represent your online persona
- ♠ Spreads Razz

Hits

- ♠ Frequent player points scheme
- ♠ Regular opportunities to play with the pros
- ♠ Lobby information includes players/flop and hands/hour
- ♠ Instant recaps of past hands

Misses

- ♠ No telephone support

Review

Introduction

Full Tilt Poker is one of a host of new sites to have launched since the first edition of this book was published in early 2003. Its main selling point is that it is endorsed by a group of the world's most famous players: Howard Lederer, Phil Ivey, Chris Ferguson, John Juanda, Jennifer Harman, Phil Gordon, Erick Lindgren, Erik Seidel, Clonie Gowen and Andy Bloch, who together comprise 'Team Full Tilt'. These players are the cornerstone of an aggressive and highly professional marketing campaign. Indeed, you can even play against them on the site if you wish to rub shoulders with the top pros! (These players are highlighted in red in case you want to seek them out or avoid them!)

In July 2005, many of the Team Full Tilt players (together with Daniel Negreanu and several other professionals) met in a special made-for-TV $500,000 tournament, which was broadcast live on Fox Sports Net.

Software and Graphics

The site has its own, very attractive software. When you sign up you can choose from a range of avatars to represent you at your seat on the table, ranging from a shark to a cowboy to a chicken. These avatars even have different expressions: happy, sad, confused etc. Overall, the game play is slick, visually attractive and enjoyable. Furthermore, the lobby is very well designed, with all the information you could wish for.

One interesting innovation is the 'last hand' feature, which enables you to backtrack and see the showdowns of past hands in a visually intuitive way.

Game Variety

Full Tilt Poker has a very wide range of cash games and tournaments. In addition to the standard fare, it is also one of the few places where razz (and no-limit Omaha hi/lo) is spread.

The ring games are nine players rather than the usual ten. In general, most players prefer the ten-player tables for the following reasons:

♠ The hourly rake is cheaper when it is split between ten players rather than nine.

♠ The blinds don't come around quite as quickly with ten players.

♠ Often with one or two players sitting out and/or players leaving the game, a nine-player table can become quite short-handed.

♠ Waiting times are likely to be shorter for ten-player games, since there is one extra player who might leave the table.

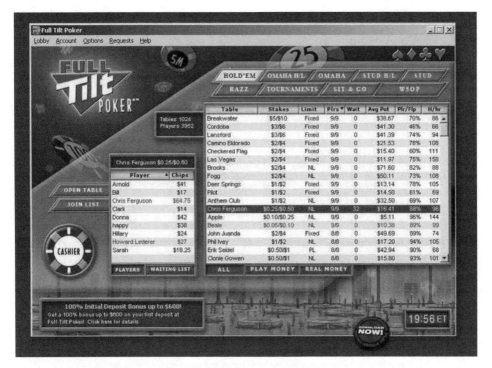

Site Traffic

Full Tilt Poker has done a successful job of attracting to players during its launch period. At peak times it currently has around 1000 real money players and 2500 tournament players.

Customer Support

The site handles support issues via e-mail. There is no telephone support or live hosts. However, the support team has a good reputation.

Rakes and Tournament Registration Fees

Full Tilt Poker has fairly standard rakes and registration fees. The rake for the larger games is taken every $20, which makes it relatively expensive. However, the heads-up games are raked at a very competitive $0.50 maximum.

Promotions and Special Events

The site has a good range of promotions, which include tournament bounties for knocking out the pros. At the time of writing Full Tilt Poker is offering a remarkable 100% matching deposit bonus up to $600.

Website

The Full Tilt Poker website is kept bang up-to-date. There were even live updates from the 2005 World Series of Poker. Furthermore, there are regular additions to the 'tips from the pros' section.

Rating

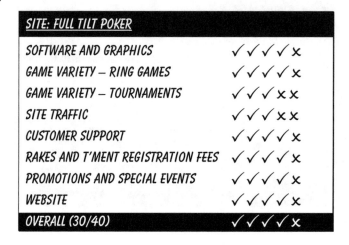

SITE: FULL TILT POKER	
SOFTWARE AND GRAPHICS	✓✓✓✓✗
GAME VARIETY – RING GAMES	✓✓✓✓✗
GAME VARIETY – TOURNAMENTS	✓✓✓✗✗
SITE TRAFFIC	✓✓✓✗✗
CUSTOMER SUPPORT	✓✓✓✓✗
RAKES AND T'MENT REGISTRATION FEES	✓✓✓✓✗
PROMOTIONS AND SPECIAL EVENTS	✓✓✓✓✗
WEBSITE	✓✓✓✓✗
OVERALL (30/40)	✓✓✓✓✗

Prima Poker Network (Royal Vegas Poker)

Slogan: 'Live Poker – Real People. Real Time. Real Money.'

URL: **http://www.royalvegaspoker.com/**
(see also **http://www.primapoker.com/**)

Location: Licensed and regulated by the Kahnawake Gaming Commission in Canada

Launched: June 2002

Transaction methods: VISA, MasterCard, NETeller, FirePay, UK debit cards and Click2Pay

Special Features

- ♠ Miniview option
- ♠ Clear overview of betting to date in a hand
- ♠ Five-card stud
- ♠ No-limit and pot-limit stud games

Hits

- ♠ Toll-free telephone support
- ♠ Lobby information includes players/flop and hands/hour
- ♠ Note-taking and statistics functions

Misses

- ♠ Fairly basic software
- ♠ No seven-card stud hi/lo
- ♠ No frequent player points scheme

Review

Introduction

The Prima Poker network comprises dozens of cardrooms, all feeding into the same games. We have chosen to focus on Royal Vegas Poker here, since it is a typical skin. Other major Prima Poker skins include:

http://www.32redpoker.com/

http://www.7sultanspoker.com

http://www.bet365poker.com

http://www.gamingclubpoker.com/

Royal Vegas Poker is part of Fortune Lounge, one of the oldest and largest online casino groups. (Another Prima Poker network site, 7Sultans Poker, is also part of the same group).

The shuffle at Prima Poker is regularly reviewed by PriceWaterhouseCoopers Inc, and no props are employed on the network.

Software and Graphics

The Prima Poker software is provided by Microgaming (which also supplies software to Ladbrokes). This software is visually unappealing and rather clunky, but it has been significantly upgraded in the past couple of years. One nice aspect of the software is that it provides the facility to recap the flow of the action instantly through pot progression data and plate borders which show how each player have acted on every street so far. In addition, you have the option of playing via a miniview, which takes up only a part of your screen.

Game Variety

Prima Poker offers a fairly standard choice of games: hold'em, Omaha (both hi and hi/lo) and seven-card stud hi. There is no seven-card stud hi/lo at the present time, although there is five-card stud instead. Players are permitted to sit at up to three tables at a time.

Site Traffic

The Prima Poker network is one of the biggest online poker sites. At peak times it attracts around 3000 real money players and over 4500 tournament players.

Customer Support

In addition to the standard e-mail support, Royal Vegas Poker has toll-free support numbers for the US, US and many other countries. Generally this support has a good reputation.

Rakes and Tournament Registration Fees

Unlike most other sites PrimaPoker rakes in increments of $0.50

rather than of $1 for games of $2/$4 and above. This means that players will pay a lot more rake over time.

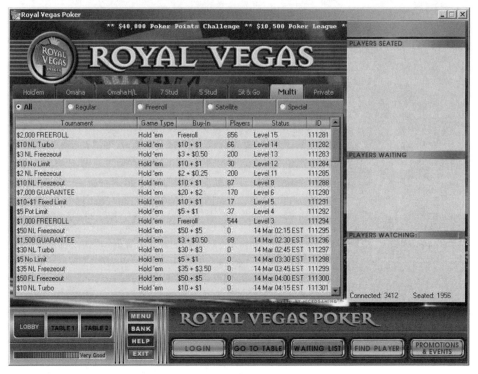

Promotions and Special Events

In November 2004, Prima Poker sponsored the first Monte Carlo Millions tournament, which was restricted to online qualifiers and specially invited players. The $400,000 first prize was won by the Finnish player Jani Sointula. The 2005 event promised to be even better, with a guaranteed $1,000,000 for first place.

Prima Poker also sponsors the Hendon Mob, a popular group of four English professionals who play in all the major tournaments around the world on the 'Prima Poker Tour'. As part of the sponsorship, the site sometimes runs 'Beat the Mob' tournaments, in which a bounty is awarded to each player to eliminate one of the Hendon Mob.

There are also currently two freeroll tournaments every day.

Website

The Royal Vegas Poker website has all the basic information about the site, but no extra topical content which would encourage players to return to the website on a regular basis.

Rating

SITE: PRIMA POKER NETWORK (ROYAL VEGAS POKER)	
SOFTWARE AND GRAPHICS	✓✓✓ ✗✗
GAME VARIETY – RING GAMES	✓✓✓✓✗
GAME VARIETY – TOURNAMENTS	✓✓✓✓✗
SITE TRAFFIC	✓✓✓✓✗
CUSTOMER SUPPORT	✓✓✓✓✗
RAKES AND T'MENT REGISTRATION FEES	✓✓✓ ✗✗
PROMOTIONS AND SPECIAL EVENTS	✓✓✓✓✗
WEBSITE	✓✓✓ ✗✗
OVERALL (29/40)	✓✓✓✓ ✗

Tribeca Tables Network (VCPoker)

Slogan: 'Join the poker revolution. Everyone's doing it.'

URL: **http://www.vcpoker.com/**
(see also **http://www.tribecatables.com/**)

Location: Gibraltar

Launched: 2002

Transaction methods: VISA, MasterCard, NETeller, UK debit card and wire transfer

Special Features

♠ Frequent player points scheme
♠ Buddy list

Hits

♠ Live chat support
♠ Rake-free super-micro-limit tables

♠ Note-taking and statistics functions

Misses

♠ No seven-card stud
♠ No lobby information on players/flop or hands/hour

Review

Introduction

Tribeca Tables is an aggregated group of over 50 cardrooms, all using the same software to feed into the same games. In this review we shall focus on VCPoker, since this site is fairly representative of the network as a whole. Other Tribeca Tables skins include:

http://www.bluesq.com/poker/

http://www.doylesroom.com/

http://www.goldenpalacepoker.com/

http://www.paddypowerpoker.com/

and numerous other sites.

The Gibraltar-based Victor Chandler International is one of world's leading independent bookmaking and gaming companies. It launched its poker room in 2002. Note that for legal reasons US players are not allowed to play at VCPoker, although they are allowed on the Tribeca Tables Network at, for example, Doylesroom and Golden Palace Poker.

Software and Graphics

The Tribeca Tables software is clean, fairly fast and quite user-friendly. You can use avatars to represent yourself at the table and the site also has a buddy list and player chat in the lobby. However, the lobby information is sparse and there are not yet any seven-card stud games. You are also only allowed to play two tables at a time.

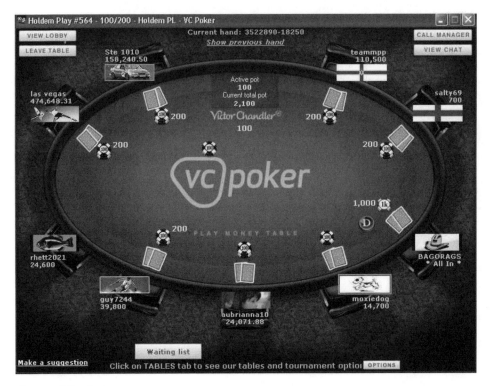

Game Variety

Tribeca Tables has the full range of standard games. Like Full Tilt Poker, it has opted for nine-handed tables, rather than the conventional ten.

Site Traffic

The Tribeca Tables network is thriving. It typically has around 1000 real money players and 3000 tournament players at peak times.

Customer Support

The site offers a good live manager chat facility, along with telephone and e-mail support.

Rakes and Tournament Registration Fees

Tribeca Tables offers an attractive rake on its $15/$30 and $20/$40: $1 once the pot reaches $40, another $1 when the pot gets to $70 and a further $1 when the pot tops $100. However, the $30/$60 and

$50/$100 games are raked at an expensive maximum $4.

There is no rake on the $0.02/$0.04 games, and a maximum $0.50 rake applies to three-handed games of $1/$2 and below. In addition, the rake structure for the no-limit and pot-limit games is very competitive. Many of the tournaments carry a reduced registration fee of 5% instead of the usual 10%.

Promotions and Special Events

In common with the other Tribeca Tables skins, VCPoker runs a frequent player reward program, 'Action Points', whereby players earn points for each raked hands in which they participate. These points can then be redeemed in exchange for tournament entries or merchandise ranging from playing cards to a super-charged Mini Cooper.

In 2004 the site organised the Victor Poker Cup, a £5000 (roughly $9000) buy-in live-action event comprising 100 pro players and online qualifiers. The first prize of £250,000 ($450,000) was the largest ever for a European event and was won by Londoner Harry Demetriou.

Website

The VCPoker website is very clean-looking and informative. It contains a good interactive tutorial, and there is even a monthly online poker magazine called *The Big Slick*.

Rating

SITE: TRIBECA TABLES (VCPOKER)	
SOFTWARE AND GRAPHICS	✓✓✓✓✗
GAME VARIETY – RING GAMES	✓✓✓✗✗
GAME VARIETY – TOURNAMENTS	✓✓✓✓✗
SITE TRAFFIC	✓✓✓✗✗
CUSTOMER SUPPORT	✓✓✓✓✗
RAKES AND T'MENT REGISTRATION FEES	✓✓✓✓✗
PROMOTIONS AND SPECIAL EVENTS	✓✓✓✗✗
WEBSITE	✓✓✓✓✗
OVERALL (29/40)	✓✓✓✗✗

Poker Room

Slogan: 'Meet them and beat them'

URL: **http://www.pokerroom.com/**

Location: Costa Rica (licensed and regulated by the Kahnawake Gaming Commission in Canada)

Launched: August 2001 (for real money games)

Transaction methods: VISA, MasterCard, NETeller, Switch/Delta and ePassporte, Moneybookers and Click2Pay

Special Features

- ♠ Available in either Java or downloadable form
- ♠ Suitable for Mac and Linux platforms as well as Windows
- ♠ Live chat support

Hits

- ♠ Fast, reliable software
- ♠ Daily freeroll tournaments
- ♠ Frequent player points scheme
- ♠ Very good rake structure for no-limit/pot-limit games

Misses

- ♠ Relatively high rakes for limit games
- ♠ No buddy list
- ♠ Unconsolidated lobby information

Review

Introduction

Although Poker Room has been around since 1999, it has only allowed real money games since August 2001. In addition to poker, the site also offers other games such as blackjack, baccarat and Chinese poker. However, residents of some countries, most notably Sweden, are not allowed to play for real money on the site. Poker Room now has several skins, including BetonBetpoker.com and Hollywood-poker.com. The latter site features celebrities such as film star James Woods and WPT Commentator Vince Van Patten.

Software and Graphics

The Poker Room ring game software comes in two formats: Windows download or Java applet (which requires that your browser supports Java 1.1). The Windows download version is very similar to other sites, but the availability of a Java version is a definite advantage both for Mac and Linux users (who would otherwise be unable to play on any download sites without Windows-emulation software) or for any players who are not permitted to install downloaded software on their PCs. In addition, users of the Java software have a choice between the standard version and a 'lite' version with lower quality graphics.

Poker Room is one of the few sites to offer keyboard shortcuts as an optional alternative to the standard mouse-activated actions. In addition, the site offers the ability to add an icon to each opponent to summarise their style of play. Another very neat feature is the fact that when a player is all-in and the cards are 'on their backs', the software states each player mathematical winning chances, and this is then updated after each street. Players are also able to chat in the lobby, without being seated at a game. The lobby information does include players per flop and hands per hour, but it is not consolidated in the main menu – you have to click on each individual table to access this data.

The site offers excellent statistical feedback on your play, including not only the percentage of times you see the flop and percentage of showdowns won, but also the average number of big bets you are winning/losing on each hand, your hourly win/loss rate etc.

Game Variety

At present limits range from $0.25/$0.50 up to $300/$600. In addition to the standard hold'em, Omaha and seven-card stud games, it is now also possible to play five-card draw (both limit and pot-limit).

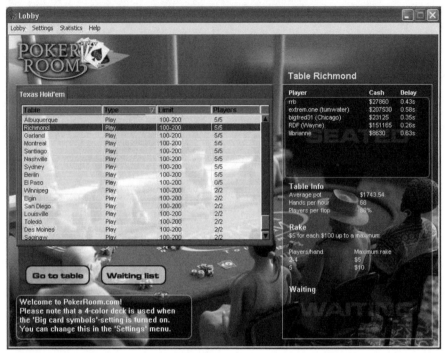

Site Traffic

Poker Room has much better than average levels of traffic, and currently ranks among the top half-dozen or so busiest sites. At peak times there are usually around 2000-2500 ring game money players, with another 3500 or more playing in either single- or multi-table tournaments.

Customer Support

The site offers e-mail based support, live chat support and (for US, Canada and UK customers) 24/7 telephone support. In general it seems to provide a good service.

Rakes and Tournament Registration Fees

The rakes charged at Poker Room are not as attractive as those at some other sites. For example, the $1/$2 game has a rake cap of $1.50 compared to $1 at the most competitive sites. Furthermore, the rake for the $5/$10 games (for example) is taken in $0.50 increments rather than $1 increments, which makes it much more expensive over time. On the plus side, the site does have far and away the best rake structure for pot-limit and no-limit games.

Promotions and Special Events

Poker Room currently runs three daily freeroll tournaments with real money prizes. It also operates a player points scheme whereby players score points for every raked hand in which they participate. These points can then be used for player points tournament buy-ins or converted into cash. One unique feature of Poker Room is that the players who score the most player points each day are awarded cash prizes, with $1000 split amongst the top 50.

Website

The Poker Room website is a core part of its operation, since it is here that users of the Java applet (rather than download) version of the software must come to access the games. It provides far more statistical information on the hands dealt at its tables than any other cardroom. Not only can you view a list of pocket cards ranked by profit (updated in real-time!), but you can also search for the results of each starting hand combination. Furthermore, Poker Room also provides a statistical analysis of 500,000 dealt real money hands, and openly invites users to conduct their own tests on raw hand history data to heck the validity of its shuffling. Poker Room also an online poker community at pokah.com, where you can find articles by well-known authors and discuss various poker topics in one of their many forums.

Rating

SITE: POKER ROOM	
SOFTWARE AND GRAPHICS	✓ ✓ ✓ ✓ ✗
GAME VARIETY – RING GAMES	✓ ✓ ✓ ✓ ✗
GAME VARIETY – TOURNAMENTS	✓ ✓ ✓ ✗ ✗
SITE TRAFFIC	✓ ✓ ✓ ✓ ✗
CUSTOMER SUPPORT	✓ ✓ ✓ ✓ ✗
RAKES AND T'MENT REGISTRATION FEES	✓ ✓ ✗ ✗ ✗
PROMOTIONS AND SPECIAL EVENTS	✓ ✓ ✓ ✗ ✗
WEBSITE	✓ ✓ ✓ ✓ ✗
OVERALL (28/40)	✓ ✓ ✓ ✗ ✗

Ladbrokes

Slogan: 'Europe's busiest poker site'

URL: http://www.ladbrokespoker.com/

Location: Gibraltar

Launched: May 2002 (for real money games)

Transaction methods: VISA, MasterCard, NETeller, UK debit cards, Western Union, wire transfer, money order, bank draft, personal cheque and cashier's cheque

Special Features

- ♠ Miniview option
- ♠ Clear overview of betting to date in a hand
- ♠ Five-card stud
- ♠ No-limit and pot-limit stud games

Hits

- ♠ Telephone support
- ♠ Lobby information includes players/flop and hands/hour
- ♠ Note-taking and statistics functions
- ♠ Part of globally respected brand

Misses

- ♠ Unavailable to US residents
- ♠ Fairly basic software
- ♠ No seven-card stud hi/lo
- ♠ No frequent player points scheme

Review

Introduction

Launched in May 2002, the Ladbrokes poker site quickly became a major player. Whereas most other start-up sites face an ongoing struggle to convince potential new clients of their credibility, Ladbrokes has no such problems. The company is one of the world's oldest and most successful sports books, with high street bookmaking shops throughout the UK, and is part of the globally-famous hotel and casino brand Hilton Group plc. According to Morgan Stanley (as reported in an article on FT.com, the online version of the British *Financial Times*) the casino at Ladbrokes.com was already valued at $500m in February 2002, even before their poker site was launched later in the spring.

The Ladbrokes site runs on the same Microgaming software that is used by the Prima Poker network, although the games themselves are not connected in any way. Under the terms of their agreement, Microgaming receives a monthly royalty fee from revenue generated by the Ladbrokes cardroom.

Unlike the situation with most Internet gambling sites, UK credit card companies do in general accept transactions with Ladbrokes. Furthermore, Ladbrokes does not charge any exchange rate fees, so you receive the same rate when you cash-out as when you buy-in (unless the exchange rate has moved in the meantime).

The shuffle at Ladbrokes is reviewed by PriceWaterhouseCoopers Inc, and the site does not employ props to help support its games.

Software and Graphics

The software at Ladbrokes is visually unappealing and rather clunky, but it has been significantly upgraded in the past couple of years. Like Prima Poker, Ladbrokes provides the facility to recap the flow of the action instantly through pot progression data and plate borders. In addition, you have the option of playing via a miniview, which takes up only a part of your screen. Players are allowed to play up to three tables.

Unfortunately, players from the US are barred from Ladbrokes 'due to the complexities of the legal issues surrounding betting in the United States' (according to customer services). However, if you are actually able to play at the site, then you should be able to find a game at Ladbrokes at times when other sites are experiencing little traffic, since the absence of US-based players means that peak times here are different to all of the other major sites.

Another side-effect of the exclusion of US players is that the site is more Eurocentric in its game selection. Whereas limit poker is the traditional game in the US, most European players are brought up on pot-limit and no-limit poker. Hence the pot-limit and no-limit games (which go up to $25/$50, some of the highest on the Internet) at Ladbrokes are usually well-supported, and there is comparatively little action in the $3/$6 to $20/$40 range of limit games. However, low-limit games below that range are quite popular (and loose!), and Ladbrokes actually spreads some of the highest limit ring games on the web, $100/$200, $200/$400 and $300/$600.

Game Variety

Ladbrokes offers a fairly standard choice of games: hold'em, Omaha (both hi and hi/lo) and seven-card stud hi. However, there is no seven-card stud hi/lo at the present time, although there is five-card stud instead. There are both single-table and multi-table tournaments, but the latter were restricted to hold'em when I checked them out.

Site Traffic

Despite the absence of US players, Ladbrokes has a strong player base. At peak times there are typically around 1300-1800 cash players on the site, with a further 3000-4000 competing in tournaments. There is not much Omaha hi/lo or stud action on the site.

Customer Support

Ladbrokes provides an online help facility and telephone support number alongside its e-mail support. However, when the site first launched there were a great deal of teething problems relating to support issues.

Rakes and Tournament Registration Fees

The maximum rake for the all tables at Ladbrokes is $3, which makes it a very expensive place to play short-handed or micro-limit games.

Regular weekly tournament buy-ins range from $5 to $500. The $1 charge for the $5 events is poor value, but there is no charge for the $1 buy-in events. There are also freeroll tournaments every day.

Promotions and Special Events

Ladbrokes has always been very active in bringing players from online games to the live-action' arena. In December 2002, two Ladbrokes players (Jonny Akesson and Alan Mudd) won online satellites to qualify for the 36-player 'Poker Million Masters', with a first prize of $150,000 and a total prize fund of $360,000. The tournament, which also included 1999 WSOP Champion Noel Furlong, WSOP bracelet-holder Dave 'Devilfish' Ulliott and the winner of the first 'Poker Million', John Duthie, was broadcast on Sky Sports in the UK in the spring of 2003. Despite good performances, neither online qualifier managed to make it through to the six-player final. However, the 'Ladbrokes Poker Million', as it is now known, has since gone from strength to strength, and Ladbrokes added a whopping $1.25 million to the 2005 prize pool.

The first Ladbrokes poker cruise took place in late 2004. The maiden voyage across the Mediterranean ended in victory for 74-year-old veteran Eric Dalby. Having entered the competition via a $2 online qualifier, Eric walked off with a first prize of $250,000. The second Ladbrokes poker cruise was scheduled to take place in the Caribbean in January 2006.

In April 2005 Ladbrokes organised the first European Online Championship of Poker (LEOCOP), which included a $2500 buy-in main event with a prize fund of over $1 million.

Website

The Ladbrokes website was recently upgraded, and it is now updated on a consistent basis. The site also has some interesting diary pieces on the European scene, penned by its sponsored player, 2002 World Heads-Up runner-up Roy 'The Boy' Brindley.

Rating

SITE: LADBROKES	
SOFTWARE AND GRAPHICS	✓✓✓✗✗
GAME VARIETY – RING GAMES	✓✓✓✓✗
GAME VARIETY – TOURNAMENTS	✓✓✓✓✗
SITE TRAFFIC	✓✓✓✓✗
CUSTOMER SUPPORT	✓✓✓✗✗
RAKES AND T'MENT REGISTRATION FEES	✓✗✗✗✗
PROMOTIONS AND SPECIAL EVENTS	✓✓✓✓✗
WEBSITE	✓✓✓✓✗
OVERALL (27/40)	✓✓✓✗✗

CryptoLogic Network (William Hill Poker)

Slogan: 'The smart players know where the big money is'

URL: **http://www.williamhillpoker.com/** (see also **http://www.cryptologic.com/** and **http://www.wagerlogic.com/**)

Location: Licensed in the UK

Launched: January 2003

Transaction methods: VISA, MasterCard, NETeller, UK debit cards, Western Union, wire transfer and personal cheque

Special Features

♠ Progressive bad beat jackpot

Hits

♠ Monthly bonuses
♠ Telephone support
♠ Lobby information includes players/flop and hands/hour

Misses

♠ Very high rakes
♠ Clunky software

Review

Introduction

The CryptoLogic network is an aggregation of ten cardroom 'skins', all sharing the same player base. In this review, we shall focus on one of these skins, William Hill Poker, since this site is representative of the network as a whole. Other CryptoLogic skins include:

http://www.intercasinopoker.com/

http://www.caribbeansunpoker.com/

http://www.betfairpoker.com/

and several other sites.

William Hill is a well-established name in British bookmaking, with over 65 years of experience in providing legal betting services and over 1500 licensed betting offices in the UK alone. It is therefore a highly reputable operation.

Software and Graphics

The CryptoLogic software is quite slow and rather clunky-looking. When the network first launched I experienced more disconnections here than I have had at any other site. Furthermore, it was very difficult to get back into a game once you had been disconnected. On the plus side, the lobby information is very good, including hands per hour and players per flop.

Game Variety

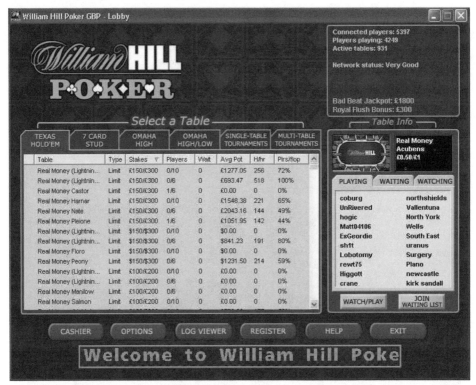

The standard fare of games is available, except that there are no seven-card stud hi/lo games.

Site Traffic

The CryptoLogic network has good traffic levels, with over 1500 real money players and around 2500 tournament players at peak times.

Customer Support

Both telephone and e-mail support is available. Overall Customer support has a fairly average reputation, with quite slow response times.

Rakes and Tournament Registration Fees

The rake is set at 5% up to a maximum of $3 (or £3 if you are playing in a pounds sterling game rather than a US dollar game). Of course, this means that is highly inadvisable to play in the pounds sterling games, since the rake is then capped at a hefty £3 (over $5)! In addition, the rake is extracted at £0.25 (or $0.25) intervals, which is by far the worst rake structure of any major site. Finally, the rake for heads-up games goes up to $2 ($2) for $10/$20, which is also very competitive.

In addition, you are charged £2 per month from the balance of your account if your account becomes dormant (i.e. you don't play or make a transaction that month).

Promotions and Special Events

In December 2004 the CryptoLogic network organised the first 'Caribbean Poker Classic' in St Maarten, which attracted 47 direct buy-ins in addition to the 110 online qualifiers. The first prize of over $200,000 was won by a Betfairpoker qualifier, John Earle from Essex, UK. The second Caribbean Poker Classic was scheduled to take place in St Kitts in late 2005.

At William Hill Poker players receive a £5 (roughly $9) bonus for every hour they play in cash games, up to a maximum of £25 (roughly $45) per month. In addition, from time to time the site requests you to move to a specified table to play as a temporary prop, for which you are financially remunerated. There is also a progressive bad beat jackpot, and a generous reward for anyone who is fortunate enough to make a royal flush (using both hole cards).

Website

The William Hill Poker website is quite slick-looking and informative. It incorporates the monthly newsletter, *Poker Times*, which contains articles by both regular players and sponsored professionals.

Rating

SITE: CRYPTOLOGIC NETWORK (WILLIAM HILL POKER)	
SOFTWARE AND GRAPHICS	✓✓✗✗✗
GAME VARIETY – RING GAMES	✓✓✓✗✗
GAME VARIETY – TOURNAMENTS	✓✓✓✓✗
SITE TRAFFIC	✓✓✓✓✗
CUSTOMER SUPPORT	✓✓✓✗✗
RAKES AND T'MENT REGISTRATION FEES	✗✗✗✗✗
PROMOTIONS AND SPECIAL EVENTS	✓✓✓✓✗
WEBSITE	✓✓✓✓✗
OVERALL (24/40)	✓✓✓✗✗

True Poker

Slogan: 'The real deal™'

URL: http://www.truepoker.com/

Location: Antigua

Launched: May 2001 (for real money games)

Transaction methods: VISA, MasterCard, NETeller, PrePaid ATM, bank draft and cashier's cheque

Special Features

- ♠ Unique 3D real-game simulation
- ♠ Select from a range of animated avatars to represent your online persona
- ♠ Special sound and voice effects

Hits

- ♠ Live table hosts 24/7
- ♠ Frequent player points scheme
- ♠ Shortcut 'hot' keys for each action
- ♠ Lobby information includes players/flop

Misses

- ♠ No seven-card stud
- ♠ Rather slow gameplay

Review

Introduction

True Poker has taken a rather unique approach to online poker, aiming to provide an online 'real poker experience' using real-life effects. Indeed many players enjoy the True Poker environment, which is less impersonal than most other sites. However, given the resource-hungry nature of their graphics, games at the True Poker have always been relatively slow by industry standards, and this has discouraged many clients from playing there regularly. Recent enhancements to the software have definitely resulted in faster games, and the games are much more 'playable' than they were in the past.

Software and Graphics

True Poker's game-playing is designed to closely resemble live play, with each player represented by a talking and moving avatar, and the use of a dealer avatar who shuffles and deals out the cards on screen. When you join a game you are positioned in such a way that your perspective on the table is very similar to the one you would experience in a brick and mortar cardroom, with your avatar at the bottom of the screen and everyone else circling around in a ring.

If you are used to playing at other sites, then the True Poker game does take some adjusting to, not least because you can click on your cards to look at them and place them back on the table, and it does require more concentration to track what bets have been made at the far end of the table and see exactly where the button is. In addition, the 'realistic' feel comes at the expense of slowing down the game somewhat relative to most other online sites.

The nature of the True Poker game is such that it has a unique tell. Since players have to click on their cards to see them when they are placed on the table, you can sometimes gauge if someone has a made hand or is on a draw by whether or not they check their cards when, say, a three-flush comes on the board. Bear in mind, however, that no doubt there are some experienced True Poker players wily enough to use this back at you as a reverse tell on occasion, when they know that they have already made their flush!

True Poker is one of the few major sites which allow you to use keyboard shortcuts for your actions, instead of having to use a mouse. The site provides e-mail hand histories of your last 10 hands upon request, but you may also choose to have your hand histories written directly to your PC. Simply click on Menu > Preferences and enter the name of the folder where you want your hand histories stored into the log path. Now click on Logs > Play and check the log play box.

From the early days of its software development programme, True Poker has consulted with David Sklansky and Mason Malmuth to develop sophisticated real-time collusion prevention and detection systems. At the core of these systems is an automatically-generated 'review factor' for each client's play. When the review factor passes a certain threshold, that player is flagged for further analysis by the security team.

The complexity of the True Poker client is such that it is relatively resource-hungry and may not be suitable if your computer is extremely old.

Game Variety

True Poker has a relatively limited selection of games. Although hold'em and Omaha are available, there are no seven-card stud or other ring game tables. (Incidentally, the real-life perspective offered by True Poker does not actually lend itself well to stud, because it would be difficult to see the upcards at the other end of the table.)

True Poker does run multi-table tournaments, but they have a much faster structure than those of the leading tournament sites, such as PokerStars and UltimateBet.

Site Traffic

True Poker is another medium-sized site. At peak times there are typically several thousand players competing either in ring games or tournaments.

Customer Support

True Poker has good support options, with live hosts and both phone and e-mail support. The True Poker CEO, David Gzesh, regularly appears on poker forums to address any questions or complaints that players raise about the site.

Rakes and Tournament Registration Fees

The rake structure for the True Poker $1/$2 limit game is unusual: $1, taken once the pot has reached $12. The drop and rake structure for other limits is conventional.

True Poker tournaments have buy-ins ranging from $1 to $100. There is no registration fee taken for the $1 events, and the $10, $20 and $60 events carry the standard online 10% charge. However, the fee for the $6 tourneys is a relatively expensive $1 charge.

Promotions and Special Events

True Poker runs a frequent player points scheme, known as 'True Poker Points'. Players are awarded points for each raked hand in which they participate. These can then be cashed in for either tournament entries or rewards ranging from caps and books to a Harley Davidson motorcycle (although it seems unlikely that anyone will ever play enough hands to qualify for this prize!).

True Poker often adds to the prize funds of its tournaments. For example, in February 2003 True Poker ran a $100 (+$10) buy-in 'celebrity bounty' tournament in which, apart from the standard prizes, an additional $1000 prize was awarded to the player who eliminated renowned poker author David Sklansky from the tournament!

Website

The True Poker website contains all the details of current promotions, together with the usual information about how the cardroom works. However, there is very little topical content.

Rating

SITE: TRUE POKER	
SOFTWARE AND GRAPHICS	✓ ✓ ✓ ✗ ✗
GAME VARIETY – RING GAMES	✓ ✓ ✗ ✗ ✗
GAME VARIETY – TOURNAMENTS	✓ ✓ ✓ ✗ ✗
SITE TRAFFIC	✓ ✓ ✗ ✗ ✗
CUSTOMER SUPPORT	✓ ✓ ✓ ✓ ✗
RAKES AND T'MENT REGISTRATION FEES	✓ ✓ ✓ ✓ ✗
PROMOTIONS AND SPECIAL EVENTS	✓ ✓ ✓ ✗ ✗
WEBSITE	✓ ✓ ✓ ✗ ✗
OVERALL (24/40)	✓ ✓ ✓ ✗ ✗

Pacific Poker

Slogan: 'The best online poker room on the web'

URL: **http://www.pacificpoker.com/**

Location: Gibraltar

Launched: October 2002

Transaction methods: VISA, MasterCard, NETeller, FirePay, Switch/Maestro, wire transfer, bank draft, personal cheque etc.

Special Features

- ♠ Part of one of the world's largest online casinos

Hits

- ♠ Some of the loosest games on the Internet
- ♠ Telephone support
- ♠ Bonus point scheme

Misses

- ♠ No multi-table play
- ♠ No pot-limit Omaha (hi or hi/lo)
- ♠ Slow games
- ♠ Poor functionality

Review

Introduction

Pacific Poker is a subsidiary of Cassava Enterprises (Gibraltar) Ltd, which operates Casino-on-Net, one of the oldest and biggest online casinos. This connection means that the site does attract casino players rather than just poker specialists, which adds to the looseness of the games. (At the time of writing, Cassava Enterprises was preparing to float on the London Stock Exchange.)

Software and Graphics

The Pacific Poker software is the weakest of any of the major online sites. It has a very unwieldy look and feel, and is much slower than other sites. Unfortunately, many of the basic features which are standard to other sites are missing at Pacific Poker, e.g. multi-table play, four-colour decks, downloadable hand histories, the ability to see your opponent's hands at a showdown etc.

The lobby does include information on the number of players per flop, but, in my experience at least, this data seems to bear little resemblance to the game in progress. The information is probably too out of date to be entirely reliable for game selection.

Site Traffic

Incredibly, for a site with such notoriously poor software, Pacific Poker attracts 2000 real money players and 4000 tournament players at peak times.

Customer Support

Pacific Poker deals with its support via telephone support and e-mail correspondence. E-mail response times are often quite sluggish.

Rakes and Tournament Registration Fees

The rake structure at Pacific Poker is clearly the worst of any major site. The rake is taken in $0.05 increments, so for a $35 pot the rake would be $1.75 rather than the standard $1.

Promotions and Special Events

The site has a bonus point scheme. For every $10 you wager on raked hands at Pacific poker you receive one bonus point. Every 100 bonus points can be converted into $1, so for every $1000 you wager you are effectively receiving a $1 rebate.

Pacific Poker has recently started to become involved in live-action tournaments. December 2004 saw the first Pacific Poker UK Open in London. From a field of 108 professional players, celebrities and online qualifiers, well-known snooker player Matthew Stevens emerged to take first prize of $500,000.

Website

Although the Pacific Poker home page is fairly basic-looking, there is a good players' club section, which contains an array of strategy articles and a poker forum.

Rating

SITE: PACIFIC POKER	
SOFTWARE AND GRAPHICS	✓ ✗ ✗ ✗ ✗
GAME VARIETY – RING GAMES	✓ ✓ ✓ ✓ ✗
GAME VARIETY – TOURNAMENTS	✓ ✓ ✓ ✓ ✗
SITE TRAFFIC	✓ ✓ ✓ ✗ ✗
CUSTOMER SUPPORT	✓ ✓ ✓ ✗ ✗
RAKES AND T'MENT REGISTRATION FEES	✓ ✗ ✗ ✗ ✗
PROMOTIONS AND SPECIAL EVENTS	✓ ✓ ✓ ✗ ✗
WEBSITE	✓ ✓ ✓ ✓ ✗
OVERALL (23/40)	✓ ✓ ✓ ✗ ✗

Other Sites

There are currently well over 250 online cardrooms, so it is only possible to feature a dozen or so in detail. Here is a selection of the 'best of the rest':

Absolute Poker

http://www.absolutepoker.com/

Absolute Poker is another Costa Rica-based cardroom, and was established in 2003. The site has good bonuses and numerous freeroll tournaments every day, but has rather slow, resource-hungry software.

America's Cardroom

http://www.americascardroom.com/

Launched in October 2001, America's Cardroom was featured in detail in the first edition of this book. Despite many attractive and innovative features, the site has never really managed to amass a 'critical mass' of players and it has not become a major player on the online poker scene.

B2B Poker Network (24hPoker)

http://www.b2bpoker.com/

http://www.24hpoker.com/

Launched in September 2004, B2B Poker is owned by the Swedish company 24hBet AB. The network comprises several cardrooms, all feeding into the same shared games. It evolved out of the company's original 24hPoker site, which officially launched for real money back in 2002.

The network spreads all the standard games, along with five-card draw, deuce-to-seven triple draw and Sökö (also known as Canadian or Scandinavian stud). However, it is unique in providing spread-limit and half pot-limit in addition to limit, pot-limit and no-limit games.

Another unusual feature of the network is that instead of the standard ten-player tables, it has eight-player tables. The smaller tables are designed to create more action, but it is a moot point whether players really prefer such tables over the traditional ones. The client base is Eurocentric, which means that the site uses euros rather than dollars, and is most busy in the evening, European time.

Bodog Poker

http://www.bodog.com/poker/

It took less than a year for Bodog Poker to establish itself as the fastest-growing online poker site. Launched in September 2004, the success of this well-designed poker room has undoubtedly been helped by its close association with the well-established Bodog sports book.

The games have a very clean, pleasant appearance, and run very smoothly, and the lobby also has a great look and feel. Like at Poker-Stars, there is the facility to upload your own personalised images to place in your seat. In addition to the standard games, the site also spreads five-card stud.

BugsysClub

http://www.bugsysclub.com/

BugsysClub was launched in February 2003 using the long-established PokerPages and Poker School Online software. In the early days the 'Hendon Mob' was active in promoting the site, before it moved on to Prima Poker. To date traffic on the site has been relatively small.

International Poker Network (Total Poker)

http://www.internationalpokernetwork.com/

http://www.totalpoker.com/

Towards the end of 2002 Boss Media AB entered the online poker market with its Total Poker software. The sound and graphics at this site are among the most sophisticated of any cardroom, and one unusual aspect of the software is 'point of view' seating, giving players a realistic sight of the table, similar to that which they would experience in a live-action game. The late Andrew Glazer was a consultant on the project, and this, combined with the fact that Boss Media is a publicly-traded company in Sweden, certainly adds credibility to the site. In the past few years Boss Media has sold its poker software to numerous other casinos, and together their games now feed into the International Poker Network.

At present only hold'em and seven-card stud games are available, and not Omaha.

Planet Poker

http://www.planetpoker.com/

Planet Poker was the very first online poker site, launching for real money way back on 1 January 1998. Although Planet Poker was first out of the blocks, its market leadership did not last for long once Paradise Poker launched with its faster and more attractive software, together with a much more aggressive marketing approach. Nowadays Planet Poker is a relatively small operator with a static but fairly solid player base. (Planet Poker was featured in detail in the first edition of this book.)

Power Network (The Poker Club)

http://www.powernetpoker.com/

http://www.thepokerclub.com/

The Power Network is another aggregation of various online cardrooms, most notably The Poker Club (formerly known as poker.com), one of the oldest online sites, which has been around since 1999. (Indeed, The Poker Club was featured in detail in the first edition of this book.) The network has not yet managed to reach a real 'critical mass' of players, and traffic remains relatively modest.

PokerChamps

http://www.pokerchamps.com/

Based in Malta, PokerChamps is one of the newest online cardrooms at the time of writing. One of its founding partners is many times WPT winner Gus Hansen, who provided a great deal of input during the software development period. Currently only hold'em and Omaha hi is spread, but the other games are due to be added soon.

World Poker Exchange

http://www.worldpx.com/

The World Poker Exchange recently evolved out of WSEX poker (which was featured in detail in the first edition of this book). Like Ladbrokes, it uses a stand-alone version of the Microgaming software, and is not part of the Prima Poker network. Despite the fact that (in its various guises) the site has been around for many years, traffic is still quite modest.

Chapter Five

Using the Web

'You know you're running bad, when people keep asking you what you do for a living.' Linda Sherman, post on rec.gambling.poker

Utilising the Internet to improve your Game

There is more to Poker on the Internet than just playing Online

Whether you are a novice or an experienced player, the Internet is a wonderful tool for improving your game. First of all, the practice you gain from playing online should not only help you to achieve better online results, but should also stand you in good stead in your brick and mortar games, enabling you to make faster, more accurate decisions (although, as we have already discussed, there are various additional dimensions to live games to which you will need to pay particular attention). The sheer number of hands that you can play in just an evening of online poker means that, whether you are a beginner or an experienced player, you can potentially improve your game quicker by playing regularly online rather than in brick and mortar games.

Although the facility to play online is a key component of Internet poker, there is a great deal more available as well – indeed, even if you have no intention of ever actually playing in an online game, you will find many useful resources on the Internet to help you improve your game. Nowadays you can read articles by leading players, receive coaching online, exchange ideas with other players, find out about brick and mortar cardrooms where you can play, keep track of major poker tournaments via written reports, live audio broadcasts and even TV shows, and much else besides. In the rest of this section the various ways in which you might use the Internet are discussed in more detail. A selection of useful websites follows in the next section.

Poker Newsgroups and Forums

One of the greatest advantages of the Internet is that, in all walks of life, it breaks down barriers and brings people with similar interests closer together. The Internet poker community is available for everyone, whether they are part of an existing live-action community or do not know another poker player on the planet. The starting point for anyone looking to become part of this is a visit to one of the many various poker newsgroups and forums.

The unmonitored rec.gambling.poker newsgroup (available through any standard newsreader) is the undoubted godfather of these, having been around since 1995, when the original rec.gambling newsgroup, formed way back in 1989, was divided into individual sub-categories. In the ensuing years practically every poker-related subject imaginable has been discussed at 'RGP' (as it is commonly known) at one time or another, sometimes in very emotive fashion, since like all newsgroups, it is based on the principle of unregulated freedom of speech.

Indeed, although the uncensored nature of RGP is its greatest strength, it is at the same time its greatest weakness, since a very small minority of threads can degenerate into name-calling and abuse. However, overall RGP is a very valuable resource for the poker community – if you have any poker questions, then you are sure to be able to find the answer either by searching through the archives (available by going to **http://groups.google.com/** and then entering rec.gambling.poker in the search box and clicking on 'Advanced Groups Search' when you arrive at the RGP page), or by posting the question yourself.

Another excellent place for exchanging views and getting your poker questions answered is available at twoplustwo.com, the online arm of the Mason Malmuth/David Sklansky Two Plus Two Publishing enterprise. Here you will find around 20 different poker forums, ranging from general theory to hold'em to psychology to tournaments to Internet poker, etc. Unlike RGP, the twoplustwo.com forums are moderated, so nothing defamatory or profane is permitted, and people must register before they can post (the site currently has many thousand registered users). If you want to find other people's opinions on the best way to play a pair of pocket nines facing a raise in the small blind, then this site is probably the best place to head.

Online Reading Material

The Internet is also a great source of articles by top poker players and journalists. Here the best starting point is probably cardplayer.com, the online arm of the bi-monthly US *Card Player* magazine, whose current regular columnists include Phil Hellmuth, Tom McEvoy, Mike Sexton, Bob Ciaffone and Max Shapiro. You can typically find a dozen or more articles from the latest issue on the *Card Player* website, together with archives going back to spring 2001, so you can go back and read past columns by your favourite writers.

There are so many poker-related websites nowadays, that it is only possible to scratch the surface in a brief survey such as this. In the next section you will find many more sites that may be of interest. If that is not sufficient to satiate your appetite, then under 'Miscellaneous Sites of Interest' you will find a couple of poker portals which list hundreds more sites to explore. Happy surfing!

Poker Websites

Nowadays there are several hundred poker sites on the Internet. The following is a personal selection to help get you started. It not only contains the sites recommended earlier in this book, but also many others which may be of interest (some sites appear twice, where they apply to more than one category). All links were active at the time of writing, but are subject to change, since websites do tend to come and go.

Playing Online

The following list contains all of the major cardrooms and skins which have been mentioned in this book. See the 'Online Cardroom Reviews' section for more information on each of these poker rooms.

24hPoker: **http://www.24hpoker.com/**

32Red Poker: **http://www.32redpoker.com/**

7Sultans Poker: **http://www.7sultanspoker.com/**

Absolute Poker: **http://www.absolutepoker.com/**

Americas Cardroom: **http://www.americascardroom.com/**

B2B Poker: **http://www.b2bpoker.com/**

Bet365Poker: **http://www.bet365poker.com**

Betfair Poker: **http://www.betfairpoker.com/**

BetOnBet Poker: **http://www.betonbetpoker.com/**

Blue Square Poker: **http://www.bluesq.com/poker/**

Bodog Poker: **http://www.bodog.com/poker/**

Bugsy's Club: **http://www.bugsysclub.com/**

CaribbeanSunPoker: **http://www.caribbeansunpoker.com/**

Coral Poker: **http://www.coralpoker.com/**

CryptoLogic: **http://www.cryptologic.com/**

Doyle's Room: **http://www.doylesroom.com/**

Empire Poker: **http://www.empirepoker.com/**

Eurobet Poker: **http://www.eurobetpoker.com/**

Full Tilt Poker: **http://www.fulltiltpoker.com/**

Gaming Club Poker: **http://www.gamingclubpoker.com/**

Golden Palace Poker: **http://www.goldenpalacepoker.com/**

Hollywood Poker: **http://www.hollywoodpoker.com/**

InterCasino Poker: **http://www.intercasinopoker.com/**

International Poker Network:
http://www.internationalpokernetwork.com/

Intertops Poker: **http://www.intertopspoker.com/**

Ladbrokes: **http://www.ladbrokespoker.com/**
N.B. Ladbrokes casino is open only to players based outside of the US.

Multi Poker: **http://www.multipoker.com/**

Pacific Poker: **http://www.pacificpoker.com/**

Paddy Power Poker: **http://www.paddypowerpoker.com/**

Paradise Poker: **http://www.paradisepoker.com/**

PartyPoker: **http://www.partypoker.com/**

Planet Poker: **http://www.planetpoker.com/**

PokerChamps: **http://www.pokerchamps.com/**

ThePokerClub: **http://www.thepokerclub.com/**

Power Network: **http://www.powernetpoker.com/**

PokerNOW: **http://www.pokernow.com/**

Poker Room: **http://www.pokerroom.com/**

PokerStars: **http://www.pokerstars.com/**

Prima Poker: **http://www.primapoker.com/**

Royal Vegas Poker: **http://www.royalvegaspoker.com/**

Total Poker: **http://www.totalpoker.com/**

Tribeca Tables: **http://www.tribecatables.com/**

True Poker: **http://www.truepoker.com/**

UltimateBet: **http://www.ultimatebet.com/**

VCPoker: **http://www.vcpoker.com/**

WagerLogic: **http://www.wagerlogic.com/**

William Hill Poker: **http://www.williamhillpoker.com/**

World Poker Exchange: **http://www.worldpx.com/**

Other Online Poker-Related Sites

FirePay: **http://www.firepay.com/**
FirePay offers a free web-based money transfer service which is sup-

ported by most major online playing sites. However, at present Fire-Pay requires possession of a US bank account.

Gambling and the Law: **http://www.gamblingandthelaw.com/**
The site of Professor I. Nelson Rose, one of the world's leading authorities on gambling law, which contains some very detailed resources on the legality of Internet gambling.

Interactive Gaming Council: **http://www.igcouncil.org/**
The Interactive Gaming Council (IGC) is a not-for-profit-organisation which was set up to provide information and education regarding the interactive gaming industry.

Kahnawake Gaming Commission:
http://www.kahnawake.com/gamingcommission/
Among others, Paradise Poker, PokerStars and UltimateBet all hold licenses from the KGC, which is based in the Mohawk Territory of Kahnawake in Canada.

NETeller: **http://www.neteller.com/**
A Canadian-based online money transfer service, which is supported by most major online playing sites. With the demise of PayPal for online gambling transactions, NETeller has become the transfer method of choice for many players.

PayPal: **http://www.paypal.com/**
PayPal, the world's largest online payments service, was acquired by eBay in 2002, and ceased accepting gambling-related transactions in November of that year.

PokerPulse: **http://www.pokerpulse.com/**
PokerPulse is an independent poker-tracking portal, which covers nearly all of the major sites. It is dedicated to delivering consistent and accurate counts of money games and players, and is updated continuously throughout the day so that visitors can see which sites are currently offering the widest game selection.

Poker Source: **http://www.thepokersource.com/**
A good resource for information on all aspects of online poker.

Western Union: **http://www.westernunion.com/**
Western Union allows online transfers from the US and Canada, and is accepted by most online poker companies.

WhichPoker: **http://www.whichpoker.com/**
The WhichPoker site contains detailed, continuously updated ring game and tournament statistics for many of the world's largest online poker rooms (including PartyPoker, Paradise Poker, Ladbrokes and Pacific Poker).

Winning Online Poker: **http://www.winningonlinepoker.com/**
Another fine resource for online poker players.

Poker Magazines

Card Player: **http://www.cardplayer.com/**
The online arm of the bi-monthly US *Card Player* magazine, and a tremendous resource for all poker players. It is well worth trawling through their superb archive of past articles by leading players and writers.

Poker in Europe: **http://www.pokerineurope.com/**
The Internet version of *Poker Europa*, the monthly European magazine, which contains articles, association results and upcoming tournament information. It also has its own cardroom in association with Tribeca Tables.

Poker Player Newspaper: **http://www.pokerplayernewspaper.com/**
The online edition of the excellent fortnightly *Poker Player* magazine. Both current and past issues of the magazine can be downloaded in PDF format.

PokerPages: **http://www.pokerpages.com/**
PokerPages is another very fine resource for news and articles. It is updated with new articles, tournament results etc. on a daily basis. The PokerPages site also offers a discussion forum and 'freeplay' play money practice tables.

Poker Forums and Newsgroups

Hendon Mob: **http://www.thehendonmob.com/mobforum/**
The Hendon Mob's forum is the liveliest poker forum in the UK.

Internet Texas Hold'em:
http://www.internettexasholdem.com/phpbb2/
This forum is actually a collection of over 20 forums, devoted to everything from site reviews to bonus chasing to strategy.

Pokah! Forums: **http://www.pokah.com/forum/**
The Pokah! forums (hosted by Pokerroom.com) cover a range of topics, including online gaming, tournaments, hold'em, etc.

Rec.Gambling.Poker: **Any standard newsgroup reader**
Typically this is the first stop for anyone interested in taking part in an online forum. RGP is completely unregulated and consequently it does unfortunately attract some backbiters and spammers, though it remains a valuable source of information and debate. (Web-based access to RGP is available at **http://www.recpoker.com/** for those without newsgroup reader access.)

Two Plus Two Forums: **http://www.twoplustwo.com/**
A must for all serious poker fans. Two Plus Two publishes books by Mason Malmuth, David Sklansky and Ray Zee, among others, and their site offers around 20 popular poker forums, moderated by David's son, Mat.

United Poker Forum:
http://www.unitedpokerforum.com/forum.asp
This relatively new forum was set up in the summer of 2002 by Mike Caro and Roy Cooke.

Poker Audio-Visual

Poker-Images: **http://www.poker-images.com/**
A commercial site which contains hundreds of high-quality poker photos, available for purchase.

Poker Voice: **http://www.pokervoice.com/**
This site (run by the Hendon Mob) launched with live text commentary and a webcam from the Amsterdam Master Classics of Poker in November 2002.

Poker Books and Products

Amazon: **http://www.amazon.com/** or **http://www.amazon.co.uk/**
The online bookselling giant offers a wide selection of new and used poker titles, many at discounted prices.

ConJelCo: **http://www.conjelco.com/**
ConJelCo carries a great range of gambling books, videos, software and other products.

D&B Publishing: **http://www.dandbpublishing.com/**
The publishers of this book!

Gambler's Book Shop: **http://www.gamblersbook.com/**
The Las Vegas-based Gambler's Book Shop boasts the largest selection of gambling books, videotapes and software in the world.

High Stakes (UK): **http://www.gamblingbooks.co.uk/**
Located in Central London, High Stakes is the premier poker books and products supplier in the UK.

Poker Academy: **http://www.poker-academy.com/**
An innovative new hold'em software program which adapts to your style of play. Omaha and stud versions are in the pipeline.

Playersbooks.com: **http://www.playersbooks.com/**
This site has a huge selection of poker (and other gambling) books and products.

PokerCharts: **http://www.pokercharts.com/**
PokerCharts is a web-based application that enables players to analyse their long-run poker performance. You simply enter the date, venue, game, profit/loss and duration of each session you play; PokerCharts then number-crunches the data and produces a range of useful statistics and graphs.

PokerEDGE: **http://www.poker-edge.com/**
PokerEDGE is a huge online database of statistics for players at PartyPoker (and its skins). Subscribers to PokerEDGE are given instant access to detailed statistics on almost all of their online poker opponents.

PokerOffice: **http://www.pokeroffice.com/**
Online poker tracking software which displays real-time opponent modelling of the players you are currently facing, and enables you to assess your own play.

PokerStat: **http://www.thsoftware.com/pokerstat/**
PokerStat is a statistical database program which allows you to analyse the strengths and weaknesses of your own play (and that of your opponents) by utilising online hand histories. The PokerStat software currently supports hold'em and Omaha (hi and hi/lo) ring games and tournaments played at Paradise Poker and PokerStars, and plans to

support PartyPoker hand histories as well are in the pipeline. A free trial version is also available for download.

The Poker Store (Canada): **http://www.pokerstore.net/**
The Poker Store is one of Canada's leading suppliers of poker and gambling products. Note, however, that they do not currently ship to the US.

Poker Tracker: **http://www.pokertracker.com/**
Poker Tracker is a Windows-based program which allows you to analyse your online hold'em or Omaha play, using hand histories from your poker site. The software works in conjunction with hand histories from PartyPoker, PokerStars, Paradise Poker and numerous other sites. A free trial version is also available for download.

Wilson Software: **http://www.wilsonsw.com/**
Wilson is a well-established poker simulation software company, offering separate programs for Texas hold'em, Omaha hi, Omaha hi/lo, seven-card stud hi and seven-card stud hi/lo.

Poker Tuition

Tommy Angelo: **http://www.tiltless.com/**
One-on-one coaching from the charismatic, well-respected Tommy Angelo.

Mike Caro University of Poker: **http://www.poker1.com/mcup.aspx**
A great resource site which is packed with Mike Caro's lectures, articles and quizzes.

Bob Ciaffone: **http://www.pokercoach.us/**
Bob Ciaffone ('The Coach') is a former WSOP finalist and is the well-respected author of *Improve Your Poker*, *Omaha Holdem Poker*, *Pot-Limit and No-Limit Poker* (with Stewart Reuben) and *Middle Limit Holdem* (with Jim Brier). He is currently available for private lessons.

Poker School Online: **http://www.pokerschoolonline.com/**
Founded by Mark and Tina Napolitano in October 2001, and featuring instructors Mike Caro, Nolan Dalla, Lou Krieger, Donna Blevins, Barry Tanenbaum and Rolf Slotboom, Poker School Online is designed to provide a friendly, competitive environment for its students. Subscribers pay a monthly fee, in exchange for which they receive access to audio lessons, articles, hand analyses, tests, play money tour-

naments and other resources aimed at improving their game.

World Poker Tour Boot Camp: **http://www.wptbootcamp.com/**
A series of training camps around the US, hosted by leading players such as Mike Sexton, Scott Fischman, Thomas Keller and Ron Rose.

Brick and Mortar Casinos and Events

Aviation Club, Paris: **http://www.aviationclubdefrance.com/home_uk**
The premier French casino, stylish host of the Euro Finals of Poker.

Bellagio, Las Vegas: **http://www.bellagiolasvegas.com/**
The Bellagio is one of the most popular cardrooms in Vegas, and a beautiful place to play poker. It is owned by MGM Mirage (see also the Mirage below) and hosts the annual $25,000 buy-in World Poker Tour Championship every April.

Bicycle Gardens, Bell Gardens: **http://www.thebicyclecasino.com/**
This famous Californian cardroom (located in the suburbs of Los Angeles) hosts the Legends of Poker and several other major annual tournaments.

Binions Horseshoe, Las Vegas: **http://www.binions.com/**
The world-famous former home to the World Series of Poker.

Borgata, Atlantic City: **http://www.theborgata.com/**
The new $1 billion Borgata hotel, casino and spa complex opened in the summer of 2003. It holds over 30 poker tables.

Commerce Casino, Los Angeles: **http://www.commercecasino.com/**
The self-styled 'Poker Capital of the World' with an incredible 120+ poker tables.

Crown Casino, Melbourne: **http://www.crowncasino.com.au/**
The Crown Casino is venue for the Australasian Poker Championship, of which the Aussie Millions (AUD $1 million first prize in 2005) is the centrepiece.

European Poker Tour: **http://www.europeanpokertour.com/**
The EPT launched in 2004, and the debut season (sponsored by PokerStars) featured events in Barcelona, London, Dublin, Copenhagen, Deauville, Vienna and Monte Carlo. These events were later broadcast on Eurosport TV.

Foxwoods, Mashantucket: **http://www.foxwoods.com/**
The Foxwoods casino in Connecticut is the world's largest (so they say) and home of the World Poker Finals.

Mirage, Las Vegas: **http://www.mirage.com/**
Another very fine Vegas cardroom, located on the Strip. Part of the MGM Mirage group, which also owns the Bellagio (see above).

Rio, Las Vegas: **http://www.harrahs.com/our_casinos/rlv/**
The new home of the World Series of Poker.

Taj Mahal, Atlantic City: **http://www.trumptaj.com/**
Atlantic City's most popular cardroom, which holds over 60 tables. The Taj is venue for the US Poker Championships and was featured in the film *Rounders*, starring Matt Damon and Edward Norton.

Tropicana, Atlantic City: **http://www.tropicana.net/**
The Tropicana, which holds over 40 poker tables, is the third of the big three cardrooms in Atlantic City.

World Poker Tour: **http://www.worldpokertour.com/**
The World Poker Tour is the organiser of the hugely successful global televised tournament series. UltimateBet's Ultimate Poker Classic, the PartyPoker.com Million and the PokerStars Caribbean Adventure are all part of the tour, along with selected events from the Aviation Club de France, Bellagio, Borgata, Commerce, Foxwoods, Mirage, etc.

World Series of Poker: **http://www.worldseriesofpoker.com/**
After more than 30 years at Binion's Horseshoe, the WSOP moved to the Rio in 2005. This is the official website.

Wynn, Las Vegas: **http://www.wynnlasvegas.com/**
Steve Wynn's lavish new casino, which opened in April 2005. It incorporates a 27-table poker room, hosted by one of the world's leading players, Daniel Negreanu.

Other UK Poker Sites

Gutshot Poker: **http://www.gutshot.co.uk/**
The Gutshot is the unofficial home of the UK poker player. It hosts a thriving poker forum and now has its own live cardroom in London.

Hendon Mob: **http://www.thehendonmob.com/**
The Hendon Mob comprises professional players Ram Vaswani, Joe

Beevers and the Boatman brothers, Barny and Ross. Their website contains articles, tips, live commentaries, a forum and much more.

Miscellaneous Sites of Interest

Betfair: **http://www.betfair.com/**
Betfair, the UK's leading person-to-person betting exchange, began offering markets on major poker events with the Amsterdam Master-classics tournament in late 2002. Apart from outright winner markets, it also offers group betting and a range of other betting opportunities. Betfair now has its own online cardroom too.

Celebrity Poker Showdown:
http://www.bravotv.com/Celebrity_Poker_Showdown/
The home website of the popular Bravo TV series, which has featured such celebs as Ben Affleck, David Schwimmer, Matthew Perry, Don Cheadle, Rosario Dawson, Jeff Gordon and Heather Graham.

Johnny Chan: **http://www.chanpoker.com/**
The official site of Johnny Chan, owner of six WSOP bracelets. Content is very sparse, but the RealPlayer videos on tournament play are worth a look.

Nick Christenson's Gambling Book Reviews:
http://www.jetcafe.org/~npc/reviews/gambling/
Nick Christenson's detailed reviews are well worth checking out before you make any poker book purchases.

Annie Duke: **http://www.annieduke.com/**
The personal website of the leading female player Annie Duke, who won her first WSOP bracelet in 2004.

Antonio Esfandiari: **http://www.magicantonio.com/**
The home site of WPT winner Antonio 'the magician' Esfandiari.

ESPN Poker Club: **http://sports.espn.go.com/espn/poker/index**
Poker heads inexorably towards the mainstream! Of course, ESPN's coverage of the World Series of Poker has had a huge effect on poker's unprecedented popularity.

Fox Sports: **http://msn.foxsports.com/poker**
Fox Sports Net is broadcaster of the Poker Superstars Invitational and various other poker events.

Gamblers Anonymous: **http://www.gamblersanonymous.org/**
Gamblers Anonymous (GamAnon) is dedicated to helping problem gamblers worldwide. Since it started in 1957, GamAnon has helped millions of compulsive gamblers to overcome their illness. (Information about the UK branch of GamAnon can be found at **http://www.gamblersanonymous.co.uk**.)

Global Gambling Guidance Group: **http://www.gx4.com/**
A site dedicated to minimising the impact of problem gambling.

Barry Greenstein: **http://www.barrygreenstein.com/**
Known as the 'Robin Hood of Poker' because of his penchant for donating tournament earnings to charity, Barry Greenstein is one of the world's leading players. One intriguing aspect of the site is his in-depth series of profiles of other top players.

Phil Hellmuth: **http://www.philhellmuth.com/**
The personal website of Phil Hellmuth, holder of nine World Series of Poker gold bracelets.

Matthew Hilger: **http://www.internettexasholdem.com/**
A thriving, fun community of online players, run by Matthew Hilger, author of *Internet Texas Hold'em.*

Late Night Poker:
http://www.presentable.co.uk/html/television/television_poker. html
The official site of Channel 4's landmark TV series, which ran for six series.

Howard Lederer: **http://www.howardlederer.com/**
The personal website of Howard Lederer, one of the world's most respected players.

Daniel Negreanu: **http://www.fullcontactpoker.com/**
In 2004 Daniel Negreanu enjoyed an outstanding year, including winning best overall player at the World Series of Poker. This is his personal website.

Net Addiction: **http://www.netaddiction.com/**
A help centre for Internet addicts, which includes resources not only on Internet gambling, but also online trading, chatrooms, cybersex and other forms of compulsive Internet use.

Official Dictionary of Poker:
http://www.planetpoker.com/games/dictionary/
Michael Wiesenberg's official poker dictionary is now available online in its entirety at Planet Poker.

Online Series of Poker: **http://www.onlineseriesofpoker.com/**
A new initiative combining ten events at five different online sites (PartyPoker, UltimateBet, Poker Room, Absolute Poker and Golden Palace). The winners of each event then come face to face for the grand final.

Play Winning Poker: **http://www.playwinningpoker.com/**
Steve Badger's site contains a useful primer for online play: 'A winner's guide to online poker', and many other interesting articles.

Pokah!: **http://www.pokah.com/**
A new online poker community created by the Pokerroom.com team.

Pokenum (Poker Hand Analyser): **http://www.twodimes.net/poker/**
Just type in the cards and you can find out in seconds just how bad that beat you took was! Pokenum calculates showdown odds for hold'em (hi and hi/lo), Omaha (hi and hi/lo), seven-card stud (hi and hi/lo), razz and lowball.

Poker Calculator: **http://koti.mbnet.fi/jraevaar/pokercalculator/**
A freeware program for calculating showdown odds for hold'em, Omaha (hi and hi/lo), seven-card stud (hi and hi/lo) and five-card stud.

Poker Channel: **http://www.pokerchannel.co.uk/**
The Poker Channel launched in the UK in spring 2005, and is broadcast by satellite across Europe.

PokerPortal: **http://www.pokerportal.co.uk/**
This portal offers nearly all the poker links you could ever want!

Poker Room's Expected Value Statistics:
http://www.pokerroom.com/main/page/games/evstats/expValue/
This link provides an interesting statistical resource on all the hold'em hands played in the Pokerroom.com cardroom, sortable by hand, position, number of players and limit.

Poker Top 10: **http://www.pokertop10.com/**
A useful selection of poker top ten lists, which also provides numerous links for further research.

Poker Update: **http://www.pokerupdate.com/**
The complementary site to this book.

PokerZone: **http://www.pokerzone.tv/**
Another UK TV channel dedicated largely to poker.

Rolf Slotboom: **http://www.rolfslotboom.com/**
The personal website of professional player and *Card Player* columnist Rolf Slotboom.

Serious Poker: **http://www.seriouspoker.com/**
Dan Kimberg's (author of *Serious Poker*) site, which contains many of
his poker articles, an excellent poker dictionary and well over 30 book
reviews.

World Poker Tour TV Series:
http://travel.discovery.com/fansites/worldpoker/tour.html/
The official homepage for the WPT TV series, broadcast on the Travel
Channel in the US.

World Series of Poker, a Retrospective:
http://gaming.unlv.edu/WSOP/
A fascinating online retrospective of the WSOP.

WSOP Links: **http://www.wsop.dk/**
Links, links and more links, but no connection to the real WSOP!

Recommended Further Reading

Beginner's Books

Poker for Dummies by Richard D. Harroch and Lou Krieger (Hungry Minds 2000)

Starting Out in Poker by Stewart Reuben (Everyman 2001)

General Strategy

Caro's Book of Tells by Mike Caro (MCU 2000)

Improve Your Poker by Bob Ciaffone (Bob Ciaffone 1997)

Inside the Poker Mind by John Feeney (Two Plus Two Publishing 2000)

Poker Essays (three volumes) by Mason Malmuth (Two Plus Two Publishing 1991, 1996 & 2001)

Super System by Doyle Brunson et al (B & G Publishing 1978)

Super System 2 by Doyle Brunson et al (Cardoza 2005)

The Theory of Poker by David Sklansky (Two Plus Two Publishing 1999)

Hold'em Strategy

Hold'em for Advanced Players by David Sklansky and Mason Malmuth (Two Plus Two Publishing 1999)

Hold'em Odd(s) Book by Mike Petriv (Objective Observer 1996)

Hold'em Poker by David Sklansky (Two Plus Two Publishing 1996)

How Good is Your Limit Hold'em? by Byron Jacobs (D&B Publishing 2005)

Internet Texas Hold'em by Matthew Hilger (Matthew Hilger 2003) ***

Middle Limit Holdem Poker by Bob Ciaffone & Jim Brier (Bob Ciaffone 2002) ***

Small Stakes Hold'em by Ed Miller, David Sklansky and Mason Malmuth (Two Plus Two Publishing 2004) ***

Winning Low Limit Hold'em (3rd edition) by Lee Jones (Conjelco 2005)

Seven-Card Stud Strategy

Seven-Card Stud for Advanced Players by David Sklansky, Mason Malmuth and Ray Zee (Two Plus Two Publishing 1999)

Winning 7-Card Stud by Ashley Adams (Lyle Stuart 2003)

Omaha Strategy

Omaha Holdem Poker (The Action Game) by Bob Ciaffone (Bob Ciaffone 1999)

Hi/Lo Split Strategy

High-Low Split Poker for Advanced Players (Seven-Card Stud and Omaha Eight-or-Better) by Ray Zee (Two Plus Two Publishing 1994)

Winning Omaha/8 Poker by Mark Tenner and Lou Krieger (ConJelCo 2003)

Pot-Limit and No-Limit Strategy

Championship No-Limit and Pot-Limit Hold'em by Tom McEvoy and T.J. Cloutier (Cardsmith 1997)

How Good is Your Pot-Limit Hold'em? by Stewart Reuben (D&B Publishing 2004)

How Good is Your Pot-Limit Omaha? by Stewart Reuben (D&B Publishing 2003)

Pot-Limit and No-Limit Poker by Bob Ciaffone and Stewart Reuben (Bob Ciaffone 1999)

Tournament Strategy

Harrington on Hold'em (two volumes) by Dan Harrington and Bill Robertie (Two Plus Two Publishing 2004 and 2005) ***

Tournament Poker for Advanced Players by David Sklansky (Two Plus Two Publishing 2002)

N.B. *** indicates highly recommended